Lexicon for Lovers of Language

A Dictionary for Word Connoisseurs

Henry I. Christ

Noble House
Baltimore, Maryland

Lexicon for Lovers of Language

This book is gratefully dedicated to my wife Marie, the companion of my lifetime, without whose help and support neither this book, nor any other of my books, would have been possible.

Library of Congress
Cataloging-in-Publication Data
ISBN 1-56167-827-9

Library of Congress Card Catalog Number:
2003095315

Cover design by Tom Christ

Published by

8019 Belair Road, Suite 10
Baltimore, Maryland 21236

Manufactured in the United States of America

LEXICON FOR LOVERS OF LANGUAGE
A Browser's Handbook

The *Lexicon* has been written for the average reader who is fascinated by words and eager to expand horizons in language. It deals with everyday language situations, broadens their applications, and piques the reader's curiosity.

The *Lexicon* is a user-friendly book, scholarly but not stodgy. Everyday terms like *antonym* and *context* appear with more exotic terms like *metonymy* and *synecdoche*, but the text shows how brilliant and commonplace the words actually are. The word *chiasmus*, for example seems utterly alien, but it merely labels a commonplace device in all kinds of popular writing.

A major feature of the book is the frequent use of quotations. An opening quotation from a work of literature and frequent quotations within each entry arouse reader interest. The style is informal, light, and enriched with humor.

A glance at the contents will suggest the scope and variety of the entries. Sampling one or more entries will indicate the style and strategy.

Contents

Abstract Words

Beauty is truth, truth beauty — that is all
Ye know on earth, and all ye need to know.
—John Keats

Isn't that a lovely, high-sounding sentiment? But what does it mean? Are beauty and truth interchangeable? How can we define *beauty* and *truth*, narrowing the definitions down so that Keat's statement is meaningful to us? Probably every reader of this book will have a different reaction to the poetic lines. But talking about the sentence, communicating with others, may be difficult. "I know what it means, but I can't explain it."

The problem is that Keats has used *beauty* and *truth*, two high-powered words, abstract words without referents: things that the symbols refer to. Abstract words do not appeal to the senses. They do not refer to things that can be touched, smelled, seen, or heard. They are likely to generate lively disputes precisely because they cannot be pinned down. The higher the level of abstraction, the greater the chance of disagreement.

If we talk about freedom, one asks, "Unlimited? Are we not limited by reality, the conflicting rights of different individuals and groups?" And justice? Conflicts arise every moment in courtrooms around the world.

Concrete word are specific: *kitchen, bicycle, senator, maple*. The referents are identifiable. There is less disagreement about *courtroom* than about *honor*.

Abstract words have been the tools of demagogues and dictators. Analysis of Hitler's speeches reveals an overabundance of loaded, emotional abstract words: *fatherland, Aryan superiority, National Socialism*. East Germany, under a dictatorial government, labeled itself the *German Democratic Republic*!

The word *abstract* by etymology means "to draw from." An abstraction draws from experiences and creates generalization. That wonderful abstraction *love* arises from our experiences.

Through the years, certain experiences become associated with the word love. And so we arrive at our definition.

Abstractions are neither good nor bad. Keat's poetry is still beautiful. The danger lies in misunderstanding the misuse. Abstractions are often essential in drawing broad-based documents that must serve for long periods, not just the moment. The American Constitution is necessarily filled with abstractions.

We, the people of the United States, in order to form a more perfect union, establish justice, insure domestic tranquillity, provide for the common defense, promote the general welfare, and secure the blessings of liberty to ourselves and our posterity, do ordain and establish this Constitution for the United States of America.

This is filled with abstractions, intentionally so. The Constitution was not drafted for a year but for as long as the nation might survive. Those glorious abstract words *justice*, *tranquillity*, and *liberty* may not have exact counterparts in the real world, but by their very nature they were intended to resonate down the years. Despite the abstract words, the Constitution has served remarkably well. Amendments, interpretations, reassessments all have helped keep the Constitution current.

Abstract and concrete words give a different flavor to communication.

The voters wanted a weekly pay check, a house of their own, health insurance, college for their kids, an occasional pizza, a trip to Disneyland.

The voters wanted financial security, adequate housing, diverting recreation, and satisfactory medical coverage.

The two passages differ. The first sentence uses concrete words like *pizza* and *Disneyland*. The second uses abstract words like *security* and *recreation*. Both types of sentences are common, but the strategy is different.

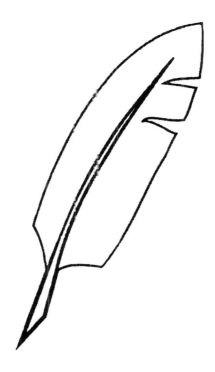

Acronym- Acrostic

NATO on Tuesday formally welcomed Russia as a participant—but not a full-fledged member—in the organization created 53 years ago to contain Soviet power and expansion.
Hendersonville (NC) *Times-News*

So familiar that it needs no explaining, NATO (North Atlantic Treaty Organization) is an example of an **acronym**, a word formed by the initial letter or letters of successive words. These common abbreviations provide easily recognized shortcuts.

Acronyms appear in all areas. A number are associated with the UN: UNESCO, WHO. Other examples include medicine: AIDS; economics: NASDAQ; space: NASA; the computer: ROM; automobile racing: NASCAR. Some common nouns are acronyms. *Radar* is derived from <u>ra</u>dio <u>d</u>etecting <u>a</u>nd <u>r</u>anging. *Sonar* is <u>so</u>und <u>n</u>avigating <u>r</u>anging. *Laser* is <u>l</u>ight <u>a</u>mplification by <u>s</u>timulated <u>e</u>mission of <u>r</u>adiation.

The word *cabal* has a fascinating history. Tradition suggests that it was an acronym for "<u>C</u>lifford, <u>A</u>shley, <u>B</u>uckingham, <u>A</u>rlington, and <u>L</u>auderdale." During the reign of King Charles II, these members of the Privy Council foreign committee often acted deviously and conspiratorially. By signing a treaty with France without parliamentary approval, they brought on a war with Holland. Even today a cabal is a group of persons secretly engaged in covert operations often to the detriment of their governments.

It's a wonderful story, but it may not be entirely accurate. The word *cabal* originally came into English from Hebrew. The qubbalah were doctrines received from Moses. The word took on its present negative meaning with the machinations of the infamous five.

Sometimes reality destroys a good story. For many years, the word **posh** was supposed to be an acronym from the time that the British Empire included India. British civil servants traveling to

India by ship preferred their staterooms on the port side leaving home and the starboard side returning home. These staterooms were on the shady side in both directions: _port out starboard home_. Unfortunately the steamship company has no record of such a usage. There are several other suggested derivations for _posh_, including linkage with _polish_.

The fish, symbol of early Christians, is associated with Christ in the Greek words _Iesus Caristos Theos Uios Soter_. The acronym provides _ichthus_, the Greek word for fish.

Related to the acronym is the **acrostic**, a composition, usually a poem in which letters, usually the first in a line, supply a name or a brief message. One of the most unexpected acrostics occurs in a speech by Titania in _A Midsummer Night's Dream_. In her enchanted love for Bottom, despite his ass's head, she declares:

> _Thou shalt remain here, whether thou will or no._
> _I am a spirit of no common rate:_
> _The summer still doth tend upon my state,_
> _And I do love thee, therefore go with me._
> _I'll give thee fairies to attend on thee:_
> _And they shall fetch thee jewels from the deep._

The first letter of lines 1-3, 5-6 and the first two letters of line 4 spell out Titania, the speaker's name. Did Shakespeare intend this? Almost certainly. Rose Eckler computed the odds that the acrostic occurred by chance and demonstrated that the likelihood was near zero.

Acrostics are an ancient form. Several Biblical psalms are acrostics- notably 119. The Roman orator, Cicero mentioned an acrostic written by poet Quintus Ennius, who died in 169 BCE. A famous example was found at Pompeii:

S A T O R
A R E P O
T E N E T
O P E R A
R O T A S

   This can be read from left to right, right to left, or even upward or downward. This may be translated as "The sower, Arepo, guides the wheels with care."

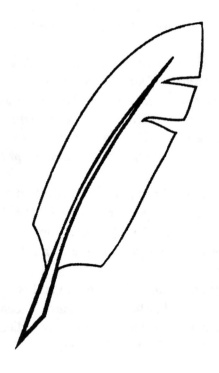

Allegory

*Now there was, not from the place where
they lay, a castle, called Doubting Castle, the
owner whereof was Giant Despair; and it was
in his grounds they now were sleeping.
Wherefore he, getting up in the morning early
and walking up and down in his fields, caught
Christian and Hopeful asleep in his grounds.*
—John Bunyan

The Pilgrim's Progress is at once a lively adventure story and an allegory attempting to teach a truth about human existence and man's spiritual journey. An **allegory** is an extended narrative using symbols to present moral or ethical values.

One of the finest examples, *The Pilgrim's Progress* follows Christian's progress from the City of Destruction to the City of Zion. Like Odysseus in his ten-year journey to reach Ithaca, Christian meets a rich mix of individuals in a variety of settings. Different from the *Odyssey*, *The Pilgrim's Progress* is a spiritual journey. Aptly named characters play the two roles: as personages in this adventure story and as symbols in a man's spiritual quest. Christian meets the unhelpful Pliant, Obstinate, and Mr. Worldly Wiseman, as well as Sloth, Simple, Presumption, Formalism, and Hypocrisy. No help anywhere there! Four virgins give him good advice along the way: Discretion, Prudence, Piety, and Charity. He passes through dangers: the Valley of Despond, Vanity Fair, and Doubting Castle, as in the excerpt. Christian perseveres. With his final companion, Hopeful, he reaches Heaven.

First published in 1678, *The Pilgrim's Progress* was a success, providing for the common reader an easily understandable vehicle for the presentation of philosophical and spiritual ideas. Entirely apart from the extended religious symbolism, the story is absorbing for its own sake, even for a modern reader.

There are other literary types related to allegory. A **parable** also teaches a moral, but is much shorter, confining itself to a less complicated message than the allegory. A **fable** also points a moral, but the characters are usually animal creatures or even inanimate objects. The fables of Aesop 2500 years ago have provided us with certain universally accepted phrases like *sour grapes*, from "The Fox and the Grapes," and "The Dog in the Manger." Later writers like La Fontaine used the fable to make a point, often sharp and biting.

> *A hungry stomach cannot hear.*
>
> *Beware, as long as you live,*
> *of judging people by appearances.*
>
> *He knows the universe, and himself*
> *he does not know.*

The allegory is not extinct. Modern versions, often patriotic, for example, show Columbia overcoming evil and preserving democracy. **Extended metaphor** and **personification** are elements in allegory.

Alliteration

An Austrian army, awfully array'd,
Boldly by battery besieged Belgrade;
Cossack commanders connonading come,
Deal devastation's dire destructive doom;
Ev'ry endeavour engineers essay,
For fame, for freedom, fight, fierce furious fray.
—Anonymous

That prolific author, Anonymous, here ingeniously creates a poem with every line alliterative and the entire alphabet covered. After exhausting himself and us at *z*, he slyly returns to *a*.

Again attract; arts against arms appeal.
All, all ambitious aims, avaunt away!
Et cetera, et cetera, et cetera.
What is there more to say?

Alliteration is the repetition of sounds in two or more neighboring words. It is an ancient device, older than rhyme. It is common in verse but also featured in prose. Many common expressions are alliterative: *bed and breakfast*, *time and tide*, *fire and flood*, *might and main*, *thick and thin*, *fun and frolic*, *tried and true*. Many reduplications are alliterative: *wishy-washy*, *dilly-dally*, *topsy-turvy*.

Poets often use alliteration for special effects. In "The Rime of the Ancient Mariner," Samuel Taylor Coleridge describes a sailing ship in graceful motion:

The fair breeze blew, the white foam flew,
The furrows followed free;
We were the first that ever burst
Into that silent sea.

Lines 1 and 3 are also characterized by internal rhymes: *blew-flew*; *first-burst*.

Edgar Allan Poe combines alliteration with onomatopoeia.

> *And the silken sad, uncertain, rustling*
> *of each purple curtain.*

The sibilant s sound provides not only alliteration but the suggestion of recurring curtain sounds.

The playful language of tongue twisters often uses alliteration.

> *Betty Botter bought some butter,*
> *But, she said, the butter's bitter;*
> *If I put it in my batter*
> *It will make my batter bitter,*
> *But a bit of better butter,*
> *That would make my batter better.*

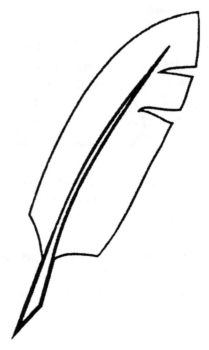

Allusion

Perhaps the self-same song that found a path
Through the sad heart of Ruth, when sick for
home,
She stood in tears amid the alien corn.
—John Keats

In his tribute to the song of the nightingale, Keats imagines all those individuals who have heard the plaintive song for generations. All those personages are nameless, except Ruth. Why choose Ruth for the example of a person homesick for the call of a familiar bird? The Biblical story of Ruth and Naomi is a tribute to love and loyalty.

Both Ruth and her mother-in-law Naomi were widowed. When Naomi decided to return to her homeland in Bethlehem, Ruth chose to go with her, leaving Moab, her own home. Keats pictures his homesick widow listening to the familiar birdsong of home. Mention of Ruth enriches the poem. Sidebar: Americans who visualize the scene are likely to have an inaccurate picture. Corn, here, is the English wheat. Ruth might stand waist high in English corn but be lost amid the towering stalks of American corn, maize.

An **allusion** is a reference to another source, often literary, historical, or natural. By bringing in a parallel reference, it adds a plus to communication. To call a person or society a *lemming* is to suggest the supposed suicidal tendencies of these rodents during mass migrations. Allusions may be so common that they are used without any thought of the source: the expression *sour grapes*, for example, has traveled far from its source in *Aesop's Fables*.

For maximum effect, allusions require a common background. Someone who doesn't know the story of *Damon and Pythias*, for example, may miss a favorable comparison with two close friends. Usually, perhaps, the meaning of the allusion is familiar, even though the source of the allusion is not, words like *colossal*, *nemesis*, or *philippic*.

Allusions are everywhere. Movie personages embody certain qualities: Charlie Chaplin- comedy; Marilyn Monroe- sex appeal; Clark Gable- masculinity. Even fictional elements from movies and television provide recognizable allusions: the Keystone Kops, the Bates Motel, Captain Kirk, Darth Vader, Forrest Gump. Each provides easy recognition.

The Bible is a rich source of allusions: *the promised land, the Mark of Cain, David and Goliath, the handwriting on the wall, Jeremiad.*

A sampling from historical events: *Waterloo, Pyrrhic victory, witch hunt, Potemkin village, Watergate.*

From literature: *Utopia, Shangri-la, Cheshire cat, Jekyll and Hyde, Faustian bargain, man Friday, Pollyanna.*

From mythology: *Pandora's box, protean, Achilles heel, Trojan horse, Cassandra, stentorian.*

From Shakespeare: *primrose path, slings and arrows, salad days, unkindest cut, midsummer madness, more sinned against than sinning, stretch out to the crack of doom.*

Whether or not a speaker knows the origin of the allusion being used, the word adds color and vigor to the language.

Alphabet

Say what some poets will, Nature is not so much her own ever-sweet interpreter, as the mere supplier of that cunning alphabet, whereby selecting and combining as he pleases, each man reads his own peculiar lesson according to his own peculiar mind and mood.

—Herman Melville

In his search for a metaphor to describe nature's complexity and susceptibility to human arrangement, Melville chooses the **alphabet**, that amazing achievement so often taken for granted. A writer selects and combines as he pleases, rearranging the letters thus reading "his own peculiar lesson, according to his peculiar mind and mood."

A superb achievement, writing is a visible recording of languages unique to the human species. It has been traced back 8000 years. Before that, primitive artists communicated information about animals in cave paintings Egyptian hieroglyphics, and Sumerian cuneiform wedges began as pictures linked to convey messages. Thus writing originated as pictorial representations, pure and simple.

A pictogram is a symbol denoting an actual object, like sun, fish, or man. Pictograms became conventionalized, often diverging from the original representation, but the essential nature of the pictogram remained. The difficulty with pictograms is the limited number of objects to draw. Language is more complicated than "two cats and a dog." (The spelling of pictograph is sometimes used for pictogram.)

Sometimes the simple pictogram might come to mean something abstract. For example, a pictogram of the Indian peace pipe might come to symbolize peace. Complications began to be introduced for even more complex abstract ideas, critical to a full expression of ideas. **Ideograms** (ideographs), for example, combine pictograms for woman and child to suggest god. For wry humor, another ideogram combines pictograms of two women under one roof to suggest trouble.

"How unsatisfactory!" a modern American might say. But the pictographic-ideographic system is a cultural blessing in many ways. China today has many different dialects, almost mutually unintelligible, but all Chinese can understand their written language. A modern Chinese can read ancient inscriptions even though they don't know how they were pronounced. Even today speakers of Mandarin and Kiangsi dialects can understand the same written message, even if they may not understand each other's spoken translation of the message.

The related word **logogram** deserves a brief mention. Pictorial traffic signs convey a simple message easily understood by speakers of many languages. Other logograms include $, %, and *. Numbers are logograms understandable to a Hungarian chef, a New Zealand opera singer, or a Norwegian sailor.

The advantages of pictograms, ideograms, and logograms are also their greatest weaknesses. They are not related to the spoken languages. There is nothing about the symbols to show how they should be pronounced. Of course, each language has a phonetic equivalent for the pictorial symbol, but the connection is arbitrary, varying by dialect. There is nothing about the symbol for *sun* to suggest how it should be pronounced. The next step called for some relationship between symbol and sound.

The Egyptians did devise some phonetic uses for certain syllables. The pictogram for the sun, re, is also found in hieroglyphic inscriptions standing not for sun but for the spoken syllable in a longer word. The Egyptians stopped there. The Phoenicians and the Hebrews took the next step. They created an alphabet. Symbols lost their ideographic connection and began to represent sounds. Though this seems logical and inevitable in retrospect, it is truly a miracle.

Proof that it was not inevitable is the Japanese language

dilemma today. The Japanese adopted Chinese characters, but they developed their own spoken language. The symbol for man is pronounced "jen" in Chinese, "hito" in Japanese. Like the ancient Egyptians, Japanese devised syllabaries in addition to the ideo-picto-grams (Kanji). These two syllabaries, called *hiragana* and *katagana*, provide grammatical functions absent from the Chinese. The Japanese, too, stopped there, short of a true alphabet.

There are two major advantages. First it provides a linkage of letter and sound. The sound of the letter *p* is now linked to the letter, helpful in meeting new words with that letter. It must be admitted though, that while this relationship is generally true, it occasionally falls to the demon English spelling. *(See "Spelling.")* American English is only partially phonetic, largely because of the growth and changes in the language.

The second advantage to the alphabet is its flexibility. In English, 26 letters can be combined in an almost infinite variety of ways. **Anagrams** *(see "Anagrams.")* demonstrate how easily the same letters can be shifted around to convey an incredible number of different meanings.

Why don't the Chinese and the Japanese adopt the glorious invention, the alphabet? On the other hand, why don't the English speakers adopt simplified phonetic spelling, like that proposed for the European Union? Inertia and apathy play a role, of course: existing books would have to be scrapped. The results might ultimately be worth it, but each new generation vetoes the idea.

Ambiguity

He is all fault who hath no fault at all.
For who loves me must have a touch of earth;
— Alfred Lord Tennyson

In *The Idylls of the King*, Arthur's Queen, Guinevere, is complaining about her husband—not for faults petty or major, but for his lack of faults, his perfection, his saintly nobility beyond the reach of ordinary mortals. Isn't this a contradiction? How is it possible, for example, to be faulty and faultless?

Contradiction and uncertainty are the heart of **ambiguity**. Two or more possible meanings are joined in the same statement or context. Sometimes the ambiguity is just plain confusing. "I'll waste no time reading your letter" may suggest an eagerness to read or a scornful rejection. Or the ambiguity may be slyly intentional. "I found the play extraordinary." Extraordinarily good? Extraordinarily bad?

On a larger scale, ambiguity may enrich a literary work. Of all writers, Shakespeare is one of the most adept at ambiguity in his portrayal of characters. Christopher Marlowe's Jew of Malta is utterly, inconceivably bad. Shakespeare created another Jew, Shylock, in *The Merchant of Venice*, but Shylock is an ambiguous character, the subject of heated debate for four centuries. "Shylock is bad, interested in money more than his daughter, willing to have another Venetian killed for revenge." "Shylock is pitiable, sympathetic, understandable, unfairly criticized." Which point of view is right? Both... and more. Shakespeare's characters, like people in real life, are ambiguous, contradictory, complicated, not easily characterized.

Ambiguity has a literary function, clarity is required in most human interaction. A ship captain's orders must be unqualified, unequivocal. A judge's sentence must be clear. A law should be easily understandable and administered fairly. Ambiguities in the wording of law can cause problems.

Equivocal, **ambivalent**, **doubtful**, and **dubious** are related words. They suggest indecision, suspicion, or lack of clarity. *Equivocal* may suggest intent to deceive. When Gravedigger in *Hamlet* parries all Hamlet's questions with unresponsive, twisted replies, Hamlet tells Horatio, "How absolute the knave is! We must speak by the card or equivocation will undo us."

Ambivalent implies simultaneous contradictory attitudes toward a person or event. Ambivalence may deter action because of uncertainty. Decisions are then most difficult when the alternatives are evenly balanced. *Dubious* and *doubtful* both express uncertainty, but *dubious* carries a negative air of insinuation.

Paradox contains ambiguity.

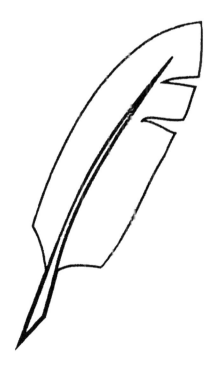

18

American-British English

To Autumn
Season of mists and yellow fruitfulness,
Close bosom-friend of the maturing sun.
—John Keats

When the frost is on the punkin and
the fodder's in the shock,
And you hear the kyouck and gobble of
the struttin' turkey cock.

There's something kindo' hearty like about
the atmosphere,
When the heart of summer's over and the
coolin' fall is here.
—James Whitcomb Riley

When George Bernard Shaw commented that England and America are two countries separated by a common language, he was bantering about the difference between American and British English. American-British differences in pronunciation are addressed in the "Pronunciation" entry. This entry provides some differences in the working vocabularies, words actually used. For the most part, the differences are not crucial. The Americans understand the British *lift*; the British understand our *elevator*.

The opening quotations suggest a subtle difference in word preferences. *Autumn* and *fall* are used both in England and in America, but in English the word *autumn* is more frequently used, as in the Keats lines. In America, *fall* is usually preferred, as in the Riley lines. A writer in *American Heritage* suggested that Americans prefer to use shorter, more bluntly descriptive terms. Perhaps there's a grain of truth in that observation but generalizations are tricky. The British prefer the shorter *pram*, *reel*, *flex*, and *braces*; the Americans prefer the longer *baby carriage*, *spool of thread*, *extension cord*, and *suspenders*.

The following lists exhibit some of the fascinating differences between British and American English. The British version is first. Answers are at the end of the entry.

A. What do you think the American word for each of these British terms?

1. lift	7. underground	13. ticket-of-leave
2. pram	8. chemist's	14. boots
3. reel	9. dust bin	15. drawing pin
4. flex	10. geyser	16. potato crisp
5. braces	11. schedule	17. vegetable marrow
6. treacle	12. wood wool	18. tram

B. If you were traveling by automobile in Great Britain, you'd come upon signs like these. What do they mean?

1. no locomotives	5. bends	9. to the chaseways
2. diversion	6. dead slow	10. dual carriageway
3. hump bridge	7. ring road	11. no stopping on verge
4. loose chippings	8. coach park	12. end of prohibition

The *telly* has familiarized the English with America speech patterns and vocabulary. TV in America has made the speech of English actors more intelligible, erasing some of the differences between the speakers of the "two languages."

Answers:

A. 1. elevator	11. timetable	3. bump at crest of ridge
2. baby carriage	12. excelsior	4. falling rock zone
3. spool of thread	13. parole	5. sharp curves
4. extension cord	14. shoes	6. low gears only
5. suspenders	15. thumbtack	7. belt parkway
6. molasses	16. potato chip	8. parking for buses
7. subway	17. squash	9. to the races
8. druggist's	18. streetcar	10. divided highway
9. ash can	B. 1. no steamrollers	11. no parking on shoulder
10. water heater	2. detour	12. end speed zone

20

Anachronism

Brutus. *Peace! count the clock.*
Cassius. *The clock hath stricken three.*
Trebonius. *"Tis time to part.*
—William Shakespeare

This striking clock is perhaps the most famous of all **anachronisms** in literature. Such clocks had not yet been invented in Caesar's Rome. An anachronism is sometimes chronologically out of place. Its roots provide a clue to its meaning: *ana- backward* and *chron- time*.

Anachronisms may be intentional. Mark Twain's *A Connecticut Yankee in King Arthur's Court* is filled with hilarious examples. Anachronisms may be a matter of indifference. Shakespeare didn't worry about such matters. He puts church bells in ancient Rome (*Titus Andronicus*), long before church bells existed. Anachronisms may be a source of error gleefully pointed out by their discovers and reluctantly acknowledged by the perpetrators.

Writing is not the only source. Films and television programs are haunted by unrecognized anachronisms that may spoil an effect. Anachronism detectives are always on the lookout for elements out of place. Automobile buffs ridicule a car used in a period before its actual production. Stamp collectors decry envelopes franked with modern postage stamps in historical films instead of vintage ones required by the script. Period pieces are especially vulnerable. A character in a Victorian play who wears a 20s dress will arouse derision.

One of the trickiest problems with anachronisms is avoiding speech patterns that developed after the period presented. William Safire devoted part of a column to expressions used before their time. A 50s movie with 80s slang will incur the wrath of the anachronism police.

Anagram

Anagrams, like palindromes, have a long history dating back to ancient times. They were invented by the Greek poet Lycophron in 260 B.C. A definitive work on the subject, placing it in historical perspective, would be necessarily large.

—Howard W. Bergerson

An **anagram** is a word or phrase created by reassembling the letters into another word or phrase. One word anagrams include *eat* for *tea*, *pore* for *rope*, and *united* for its antonym *untied*. A **palindrome**, treated elsewhere, is a specialized kind of anagram, a word or phrase that reads the same backward or forward.

The ideal anagram is one in which the created word or phrase is somehow related to the original. *Twinges* becomes *we sting*! *Life's aim* creates *families*. *Conversation* becomes *voices rant on*.

The **antigram** is an anagram in which the created word or phrase is opposed in meaning to the original. *Old man winter* becomes *warm, indolent. The Louvre* becomes *true hovel. The Waldorf* becomes *dwarf hotel*.

Thousands of anagrams have been recorded in word books. Some of the longer ones are brilliant. Here are a few examples.

Fluctuations of stocks in Wall Street.
A little luck wins; fortunes scoot fast.

Presidential elections.
I see politics enter land

Robert Louis Stevenson.
Our best novelist, Senor.

Sometimes there are two anagrams for one phrase:

Washington crossing the Delaware
He saw his ragged continental row.
A wet crew gain Hessian stronghold

A clever anagram can sum up a novel concisely.

The Scarlet Letter, *by Nathaniel Hawthorne*
Can tell thee Hester hath worn an A bitterly.

Writers have used anagrams as pen names. *Voltaire* is an anagram of the writer's actual name: *Arouet, l.j. (le jeune- the young)*. Bryan Wallet Procter became Barry Cornwall, poet. Calvinus became Alcuinus. Martin Gardner became Armand T. Ringer.

By derivation, the word *Utopia* means *nowhere*. Samuel Butler had this in mind when he titled his novel *Erewhon*, an anagram of *nowhere*. It is suggested that Caliban in Shakespeare's *The Tempest* is an anagram of *cannibal* (spelled with one *n* in Shakespeares time.)

Anglo-Saxon

Lo, praise of the prowess of people-kings
of spear-armed Danes, in days long sped,
We have heard, and what honor the athelings
won.

—Beowulf

Beowulf has been called "perhaps the earliest considerable poem in any modern language." Though it retold a legend of northern Europe, Beowulf was probably set down by an Anglian bard in the eighth century. The preceding quotation has been modernized. In its original form, the words would be mostly incomprehensible to modern readers. This is how the first line looked in the original.

Hwaet, We Gar-Dena in geardaum.

As strange as this language seems to us, it nevertheless became the backbone of the English language.

The Anglo-Saxons were Germanic tribes who lived in northern Europe. After the Roman legions had left Britain, the native tribes warred among themselves. The Celtic King Vortigern, mired in his struggles against the Picts and the Scots, asked those Germanic tribes for help. They came…and stayed, eventually driving the Celts to the west, to Wales, Ireland, and Scotland, where there are still speakers of Gaelic tongues. The linguistic impact of the Celtic language on English was slight—a few words like *bard* and *crag*, and a few place names like *Thames*.

After the Anglo-Saxons had made portions of England their home, Vikings from Scandinavia began to raid the English coasts. They found the countryside to their liking and began to settle themselves. King Alfred, Anglo-Saxon hero, defeated the Danes but they kept coming back, ultimately putting a Danish king, Canute, on the English throne.

During those troubled times, the English language began to take shape. Anglo-Saxon words, with a flavoring of Scandinavian words, formed the backbone of the language as we know it today. There were more invaders to come. England, that "precious stone set in the silver sea," was a tempting target for aggressors. In 1066, the Norman William the Conqueror defeated Harold, the last of the Anglo-Saxon kings, and established Norman rule.

This Norman-French influence had a profound impact on English language history. Instead of having only one major strand, English now had two- the Germanic and the Romance. This marriage enriched English, contributing to its incredible linguistic resources.

The domination of the French for a long period is reflected in the language. The Anglo-Saxon peasants dealt with animals in the natural state: *pig, calf, sheep, deer*. The Norman masters encountered the animals as food: *pork, veal, mutton, venison*. The infusion of French words provided a wealth of synonyms, pairs with slightly different connotations.

French is a Romance language, like Latin. The influence of Latin extended over centuries in other ways. Some Latin words came with the Romans. Early church fathers provided other words, like *temple* and *candle*. Scholars continued to add Latin roots and words to the language. Shakespeare made major contributions. Greek also provided many words for the growing vocabulary. Like Latin, Greek words continue to enter the language today. Both Latin and Greek account for more than half the words in the dictionary.

This fact is misleading. If Anglo-Saxon words are less impressive in a dictionary count, why are they important? In ordinary speech and writing, Anglo-Saxon words predominate. In a study of advertising and directional signs, words of Anglo-Saxon origin account for 70%. The percentage drops somewhat in a count of serious prose. The Preamble to the Constitution contains 25 words of Latin origin and 28 of Anglo-Saxon. Basic words of Anglo-Saxon origin tend to be shorter than words derived from Latin and Greek. In any word count, the results are tilted by the abundance of Anglo-Saxon connecting words. Indispensable prepositions and conjunctions provide the sinews of sentences: *to*, *from*, *but*, *and*. Basic nouns, verbs, and adjectives are found in any conversation: *bread*, *hand*, *good*, *low*, *come*, *see*.

Though words of Anglo-Saxon origin tend to be monosyllabic, there are exceptions. The following short words are NOT of Anglo-Saxon origin: *air*, *cry*, *oil*, *pay*, *box*, *bush*, *fine*.

Could we do without those Anglo-Saxon words? Hardly. The pronouns are of Anglo-Saxon origin. It is inconceivable trying to communicate personal messages without pronouns. How would a suitor say, "I love you" without using Anglo-Saxon words? *I* and *you* would of course be eliminated. *Love* would have to go. Hmm. Even if he substituted a word like *adore* for *love*, how would he survive without those pronouns *I* and *you*? He'd have to give his beloved a diamond ring and hope that she understood the depth of his passion for her. "I love you" is easier!

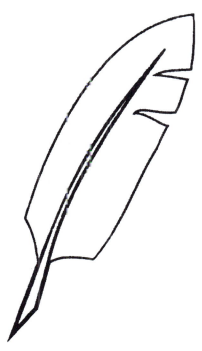

Anticlimax

Hear thou, great Anne, whose three realms obey,
Does sometimes counsel take...and sometimes tea.
> —Alexander Pope

In this couplet addressed to his sovereign, Queen Anne, Alexander Pope uses anticlimax for a humorous effect. **Anticlimax** is a sudden shift from an important or significant statement to a trivial one. Dr. Samuel Johnson, who seems to have coined the word, called *anticlimax* "a sentence in which the last part expresses something lower than the first." Pope's verse starts with a serious tribute to the Queen, a mighty ruler, counsel-taker...and tea drinker. Here the arrangement is intentional. (Note the eighteenth-century pronunciation "Tay").

The hungry judges soon the sentence sign,
And wretches hang that juryman may dine.

Here a matter of life-or-death has a bitter, trivial outcome that makes a mockery of justice.

Anticlimax may be unintentional as in this news report from the Chicago *Sun Times* (January 1, 1955).

Charges of practicing medicine without a
license, carrying an unauthorized gun, and
making an improper left turn were filed against
him.

Even Lord Tennyson was guilty of an unintentional anticlimax in Enoch Arden.

So passed the strong heroic soul away,
And when they buried him the little port
Had seldom seen a costlier funeral.

The following sentence illustrates the kind of anticlimax that may occur in hasty writing:

He rose to his feet, flung off his cloak, drew his sword, and coughed apologetically.

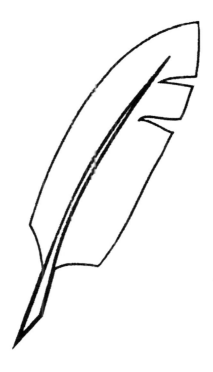

Antithesis

Crafty men contemn [despise) studies;
Simple men admire them; and wise men use them.
                                    —Francis Bacon

Antithesis contrasts words, clauses, sentences, or ideas. Here Bacon contrasts the crafty, the simple, and the wise. Abraham Lincoln was the master of antithesis. In a letter to a friend, he wrote:

> *I claim not to have controlled events,*
> *But confess plainly that events have controlled me.*

In another letter he revealed:

> *I have received a great deal of ridicule without malice; and have received a great deal of kindness not quite free from ridicule. I am used to it.*

Lincoln mastered antithesis even in a single sentence:

> *The ballot is stronger that the bullet.*

Another great President, Franklin D. Roosevelt, also used antithesis.

> *It is not a tax bill but a tax-relief bill providing relief not for the needy but for the greedy.*

> *The only thing we have to fear is fear itself.*

Winston Churchill paid tribute to the RAF in the Battle of Britain:

*Never in the field of human conflict was so
much owed by so many to so few.*

If used sparingly, antithesis can be an effective strategy, but overuse may be counterproductive. Antithesis couples surprise with recognition. Some critics feel that Alexander Pope overused the device, as in these samples.

*Be not the first whom the new are tried,
Nor yet the last to lay the old aside.*

*Some praise at morning what they blame at night,
But always think the last opinion right.*

For fools rush in where angels fear to tread.

*True friendship's laws are by this rule expressed,
Welcome the coming, speed the parting guest.*

*'Tis education forms the common mind:
Just as the twig is bent, the tree's inclined.*

*Call, if you will, bad rhyming a disease,
It gives men happiness, or leaves them ease.*

Pope cannot be accused of bad rhyming. He's a master versifier, and his heroic couplets roll on in melodic glory, easily quoted and remembered. The judgment about overkill rests with the individual reader.

Antonym

More than I, if truth were told,
Have stood and sweated hot and cold,
And through their reins in ice and fire
Fear contended with desire.

—A.E. Housman

In this stanza from *A Shropshire Lad*, Housman comments on the human condition, the emotional tumult raging through the reins (kidneys), the seat of the emotions, the passions. It's not easy to be a human being. To dramatize the range and extent of the human dilemma, he uses antonyms: *hot-cold*, *ice-fire*.

These opposing words appear in such commonplace expressions as *long and short*, *friend or foe*, *in and out*, *sink or swim*, *with or without*, *feast or famine*, *go back and forth*, *take it or leave it*. They are often used to express a wide range of possibilities. They enrich our speech by introducing contrasts "Days in the desert may be sizzlingly *hot* and the nights, uncomfortably *cold*." They help us to define: "*Parsimonious* is the opposite of *generous*." They build vocabulary by remembering that *incarcerate* is the opposite of *free*.

Some antonyms are obvious: *go-come*, *love-hate*, *succeed-fail*, *win-lose*. But a word may have many antonyms depending upon which sense meaning of the word is considered. *Dry* is a word of many meanings. We may talk about a *dry* month, a *dry* bathing suit, a *dry* writing style. Obviously one antonym will not do for all of these. An antonym of the first might be *rainy*, *showery*, or *stormy*. An antonym of the second might be *wet*, *soaked*, or *damp*. An antonym of the third might be *humdrum*, *dull*, or *stale*.

Through a quirk of the English language, some antonyms may be considered synonyms in certain contexts. *Up* and *down* have opposed meanings, but not in expressions like these: *slow up* and *slow down*, *burn up* and *burn down*. *Give* and *take* appear in *caregiver* and *caretaker*, in which *give* and *take* have similar positive connections.

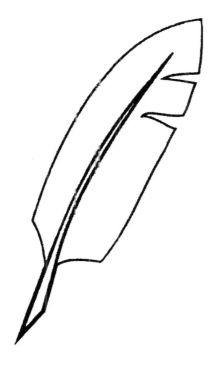

Apostrophe

Roll on, thou deep and dark blue ocean- roll!
Ten thousand fleets sweep over thee in vain;
Man marks the earth with ruin—his control
Stops with the shore.

—Lord Byron

Apostrophe is not only a mark of punctuation but also a literary device. It addresses a usually absent person or personalized object. In the quoted excerpt, Byron is addressing the ocean as if present and able to understand. The speaker may also address an abstraction. Thomas Carlyle wrote, "O Liberty, what things are done in thy name!"

Examples of apostrophe abound.

Hail, Holy Light, offspring of Heaven
    firstborn.

—John Milton

Sweet Auburn, loveliest village of the plain.

—Oliver Goddsmith

Milton! Thou shouldst be living in this hour.

—William Wordsworth

Come, seeling night,
And scarf up the tender eye of pitiful day.

—William Shakespeare

Come, mighty Must!
Inevitable Shall!
In thee I trust,
Time weaves my coronal!

—W.S. Gilbert

The word apostrophe has an interesting origin: two Greek roots: *apo* and *strophe*—literally a turning away. It is as though the speaker is on a stage and then suddenly turns away and speaks. In *Julius Caesar*, Mark Antony has been rousing his audience to a crescendo of hatred toward the conspirators. Suddenly he turns away and addresses the lifeless corpse:

> *O mighty Caesar! Dost thou lie so low?*
> *Are all thy conquests, glories, triumphs, spoils,*
> *Shrunk to this little measure?*

Perhaps the most poignant of all real-life apostrophes is said to have been uttered by the emperor Caesar Augustus. Publius Quintilius Varus, Roman general, had been appointed governor of Germany in 9 C.E. The German tribes, never wholly conquered by the Roman legions, were far beyond Varus's abilities to control. To suppress an uprising, he sent legions across the Rhine. The troops were engaged by the armies of the German hero Arminius and massacred in the Teutoburg Forest. Varus committed suicide in despair. It is said that Augustus would awaken from a nightmare, crying, "Varus, Varus, bring me back my legions!"

Although the Roman general Germanicus later defeated Arminius, the Romans never again made a real effort to absorb the territories east of the Rhine.

Aside

HAMLET. *Nay then, I have an eye of you!*
(aloud) If you love me, hold not off.

Hamlet has suddenly begun to suspect that his old friends Rosencrantz and Guildenstern have been sent for by King Claudius to spy on him. Although not specifically so marked in the text, the first line is an aside, heard by the audience, but not heard by the two courtiers. The second line is heard by the two. The **aside** is a short remark intended to be heard by the audience but not the other actors in the scene.

The aside is a convenient device, economically informing the audience of dramatic undercurrents that otherwise require more extended dialogue. By letting the audience in on the actors' thoughts, the playwright is guiding the audience's reactions to the disparity between what is said and what is thought.

Though the aside is related to the soliloquy, it is shorter and usually uttered during an ongoing dialogue. Shakespeare used the aside effectively, as have other playwrights. The aside reached its peak of popularity in melodramas of the nineteenth century. Dastardly villains expressed their evil intentions for the audience's horrified enjoyment. Because it seems to be an especially artificial convention, its popularity waned, though it has survived in experimental drama and comedy. In serious drama, Eugene O'Neill resurrected the aside for his brooding tragedy *Strange Interlude*. O'Neill was influenced by the stream-of-consciousness novel and tried to stage the inner thoughts of his characters in frequent asides.

The film has provided a technically successful use of the aside. During filmed production of *Hamlet*, for example, Hamlet's asides are delivered as voice-overs as he silently evaluates the current situation while standing motionless.

Assonance

> *In Xanadu did Kubla Khan*
> *A stately pleasure dome decree.*
> > —Samuel Taylor Coleridge

The repetition of the *u* sound in line one is an example of **assonance**, a partial rhyme in which the vowel sounds correspond but the consonants differ. Assonance is often a part of nursery rhymes and other easily remembered lines.

> *Jack be nimble, Jack be quick.*
> *Jack jump over the candlestick.*

The *i* sound is a kind of refrain.

Consonance is the repetition of consonants, with changes in the intervening vowels. These pairs are examples of consonance: *stroke- luck, mine- moan; fall- till,* and the single word *flimflam.* Rhyme results from a combination of vowels and consonants: *stroke-broke; wine-pine, fall-tall.*

Dissonance is a mingling of discordant sounds. It may be unintentional or used intentionally for effect.

> *In a coign of the cliff between lowland and*
> > *highland,*
> *At the sea-down's edge between windward and*
> > *lee,*
> *Walled round with rocks as an inland island,*
> *The ghost of a garden fronts the sea.*
> > —Algernon Charles Swinburne

The dissonance of the lines suggests the rugged setting of the garden.

Ballad

White was the sheet that she spread for her lover,
White was the sheet and embroidered the cover,
But whiter the sheet and the canopy grander,
When he lay down to sleep where the hill-foxes wander.

—Anonymous

This haunting stanza is a terse example of an old English or Scottish **ballad**. This folk ballad has roots as far back as the twelfth century or earlier. It is not a "literary" form but an outgrowth of fold tradition. It is a story in a song.

The example above is a typical ballad in mood and content. It is objective, impersonal, and dramatic. Like many other folk ballads, it leaves much unsaid. It wastes no words, leaving to the listener the conclusion to be drawn. Is it wintertime? What happened to the lovers' tryst? Why has the lover failed to appear? Has he had second thoughts? Is he dead? That's for the listener to decide.

Not all folk ballads are open-ended. Some, like the old favorite "Sir Patrick Spens," clearly delineate the shipwreck tragedy...and tragedy is a major element in the genre. Folk ballads frequently tell of heartbreak, remorse, and inconstancy. These elements will be familiar to fans of country-western music. These modern ballads use the same themes as the folk ballads, but with a difference. In contemporary ballads, the plaint is more personal. The pronoun I gives the singer's side of the story. Folk ballads, like good journalists, report the narrative more objectively and impersonally.

Although unrequited love plays a role in folk ballads, other subjects include adventure, deeds of prowess, supernatural happenings, and even humor, as in the masterpiece "Get Up and Bar the Door." In this ballad the wife is making puddings as a strong wind blows open the door of their home. The husband says to his wife, "Get up and bar the door." "You do it," she replies. "I'm busy." He refuses. They make a pact that the first person to speak must bar the door.

The plot thickens. Robbers enter through the open door and begin to take liberties, even asserting that they'll kiss the wife. This is too much for the husband.

> O up then started our Goodman,
> An angry man was he:
> "Will you kiss my wife before my eyes,
> And scald me with puddingbree?"
>
> Then up and started our good wife,
> Gave three skips on the floor:
> "Goodman, you've spoken the foremost word.
> Get up and bar the door."

A homely little drama, told with humor and insight, without a wasted word.

The literary ballad attempts to capture the power of the folk ballad. A stanza from Coleridge's *The Ancient Mariner* provides a good example.

> Day after day, day after day,
> We stuck, nor breath nor notion;
> As idle as a painted ship
> Upon a painted ocean.

As the Mariner constantly interjects his feelings and regrets, the ballad loses impersonality and departs from the folk tradition. The literary ballad was favored by other poets, among them Wordsworth, Keats, and Tennyson.

Except for the opening stanza, the examples in this entry are examples of the ballad stanza. The opening stanza uses heroic couplets *(see "Couplets")*, but the usual ballad stanza consists of four lines: four poetic feet alternating with three *(see "Meter")*. Usually the second and fourth lines rhyme. With its strong rhyme and simple structure, the ballad stanza has always been a favorite to express emotion or tell a story.

The word ballad is also used as a general word for a popular song.

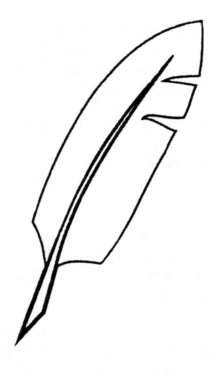

Carpe Diem

Gather ye rosebuds while ye may;
Old Time is still a-flying;
And this same flower that blooms today,
Tomorrow will be dying.
>   —Robert Herrick

Carpe diem! Seize the day! Life is short. Enjoy yourself while you can. Herrick's poem expresses the theme concisely. It appears throughout literature. Christopher Marlowe's passionate shepherd urges his love:

Come live with me and be my love,
And we will all the pleasures prove.

There is always a flip side to the carpe diem impulse. Sir Walter Raleigh turned a cold and practical eye on the invitation:

If all the world and love were young,
And truth in every shepherd's tongue,
These pretty pleasures might me move,
To live with thee and by thy love.

Conflicting impulses and philosophies are inevitable in literature and in life. The carpe diem philosophy has sometimes been called the "motto of **Epicureanism**," named after an ancient Greek philosopher. Although Epicurus upheld pleasure as the end of all morality, he emphasized that real pleasure can be attained "through a life of prudence, honor, and justice." Epicureanism is sometimes loosely and unfairly paired with **Hedonism**, the pursuit of pleasure by total gratification of the senses. Epicureanism as originally practiced insisted that pleasure is the absence of pain, achieved through rational control of desire.

Epicureanism has sometimes been contrasted with **Stoicism**, briefly defined as "indifference to pleasure or pain." Although this is a deceptively simple explanation of a complex philosophy, it is illuminating. Stoics accept joy and treasure impassively, accepting whatever happens as the will of the gods. The Stoics were among the most important men of the ancient times. Virtue was the highest good, identified with happiness, untouched by changes in fortune.

Hamlet expresses the Stoic ideal in his tribute of Horatio:

> *Thou hast been*
> *As one in suff'ring all that suffers nothing,*
> *A man that Fortune's buffets and rewards*
> *Hast ta'en with equal thanks, and blest are those*
> *Whose blood and judgment are so well commingled*
> *That they are not a pipe for Fortune's finger*
> *To sound what stop she please; give me that man*
> *That is not passion's slave, and I will wear him*
> *In my heart's core, Aye, in my heart of heart,*
> *As I do thee.*

The Stoic philosophy has never been expressed more eloquently and passionately.

Interesting etymology: *stoic* comes from *stoa*, or *porch*, where the philosopher Zeno taught.

Related partially to the Stoics were the **Cynics**. They taught a life of self-sufficiency, suppression of desires, restriction of wants. They glorified poverty and negativity. Theirs was a selfish philosophy, indifferent to others.

The name most closely associated with the Cynics was Diogenes, whose major claim to fame was his fruitless search by day, lantern in had, for an honest man. Diogenes was a Cynic to the core. He lived in a tub, threw away a drinking cup when he saw a peasant cupping his hands for a drink. When the conqueror Alexander the Great asked what he might do for him, Diogenes said "Only step out of my daylight." His complete contempt for his generation was echoed in Shakespeare's character Timon of

Athens.

The four philosophies described here still influence modern thought and action.

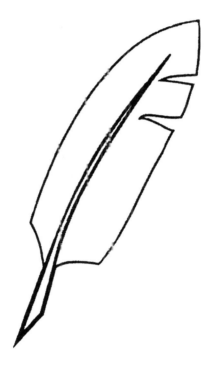

Chiasmus

Ask not what your country can do for you;
ask what you can do for your country.
—John F. Kennedy

Kennedy's famous line in his Inaugural Address illustrates a common linguistic device: **chiasmus**. It's surprising that so many common linguistic devices have forbidding names, like *metonymy*, *synecdoche*, and *syntax*. Chiasmus is another common device, familiar to everyone.

The word has a Greek root based upon the letter *chi*, for "crossing." One dictionary defines *chiasmus* as "a rhetorical inversion of the second of two parallel structures." The Kennedy quotation inverts the sentence, transferring the obligation from the country to the individual. As author Mardy Grothe points out, chiasmus has been used by writers as diverse as Winston Churchill and Will Rogers, William Shakespeare and Dorothy Parker, Ben Franklin and Mark Twain.

Both the Old and New Testaments of the Bible abound in chiasmus. The Greeks of Periclean Athens used it:

It is not the oath that makes us believe the man,
But the man the oath.

—Aeschylus

Bad men live that they may eat and drink,
whereas good men eat and drink that they may live.

—Socrates

Other philosophers have loved chiasmus:

Failure is the foundation of success;
success is the lurking place of failure.
—Lao-tzu

The art of progress is to preserve order amid change,
and to preserve change amid order.
—Alfred North Whitehead

It is as hard for the good to suspect evil
as it is for the evil to suspect good.
—Cicero

It a man will begin with certainties,
he shall end up in doubts;
but if he will be content to begin with doubts,
he shall end up in certainties
—Francis Bacon

Wordly advice is often provided in the form of chiasmus:

Never be haughty to the humble;
never be humble to the haughty
—Jefferson Davis

Take care to get what you like
or you will be forced to like what you get.
—George Bernard Shaw

The earth does not belong to man;
man belongs to the earth.
—Chief Seattle

When you have nothing to say,
say nothing.
—Charles Caleb Colton

Chiasmus provides a superb vehicle for wordplay and witticism:

It's not the men in my life,
it's the life in my men.

—Mae West

Never let a fool kiss you,
or a kiss fool you.

—Joey Adams

Recreational wordplayers wonder why
we drive on a parkway
and park on a driveway.

—Richard Lederer

Better a witty fool
than a foolish wit.

—William Shakespeare

One of the most famous examples of chiasmus arose in London in 1728. The satirist Jonathan Swift gave his friend John Gay the idea for a musical play set largely in Newgate prison and dealing with some attractive, if unsavory, characters. After a series of rejections, Gay took his masterpiece, *The Beggar's Opera*, to the producer John Rich, who saw its potential. It became a sensational success. London wits made the comment: "It made Rich gay and Gay rich."

The force of the comment is somewhat diluted by the changing use of the word *gay*.

Shakespeare used chiasmus to conclude the final sonnet in his immortal sonnet sequence:

Love's fire heat water, water cools not love.

Classification

"When I use a word," Humpty Dumpty said, in a rather scornful tone, "it means just what I choose it to mean—neither more nor less."

"The question is," said Alice, "whether you can make words mean so many different things."

"The question is," said Humpty Dumpty, "which is to be master— that's all."

—Lewis Carroll

In his sharp dialogue with Alice in *Through the Looking Glass*, Humpty Dumpty proves himself to be a student of language who understands the function of words. Words in themselves don't "mean" anything. They acquire agreed-upon meanings through the contrasts accepted by all members of the language community. This simple truth is largely ignored in heated disputes, family wrangles, and diplomatic doublespeak.

Language sets up categories, essential for human interaction, but the categories exist inside heads, not "out there." **Classification** of horses, motorcycles, nuclear missiles, houses, poisonous plants, is essential for personal and society's survival. But the classifications are not rigid; they do not exist in the real world. They change. They are understood differently by different persons at different times under different circumstances. Classification enables a society to survive…and sometimes to destroy itself.

Language is a magnificent human achievement, but its incredible strength is paradoxically its greatest weakness. The word is not the thing. A tomato is a fruit, a vegetable, a natural work of art, a decorative element, an allergenic food for some persons. What is it anyway? The answer depends upon the speaker and the context-but all answers are necessarily verbal: a game within a game. As Humpty Dumpty suggested, words mean what we choose them to mean.

The power of words is crucial in primitive societies. Magic chants influence behavior. Modern, supposedly sophisticated society is affected in similar ways. Modern magic chants include political slogans, team victory cries, advertising jingles. The magic word *free* gets everyone's attention. *New and improved* sounds great but may conceal a slight change in the product and a reduction in the weight of that product. The contents of the cereal box may not reflect the claim on the cover.

A football team would rather be called the *Tigers* than the *Pals*. In selling a coat, the advertiser may prefer to use *stylish*, rather than *sturdy*. A *garden-fresh* salad somehow tastes better than just *a salad*.

Law, medicine, education, politics, diplomacy—all aspects of life depend upon setting up useful categories. The danger is believing that these categories exist outside human consciousness.

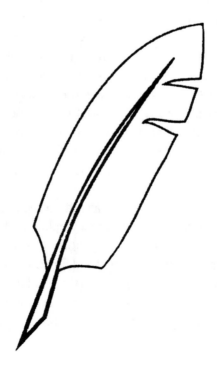

Cliché

Where'er you find "the cooling western breeze."
In the next line it "whispers through the trees;"
If crystal streams "with pleasing murmurs creep,"
The reader's threatened (not in vain) with sleep.
— Alexander Pope

Nearly three hundred years ago in his *Essay on Criticism* Alexander Pope poked fun at expressions that had been worn threadbare usually by poets, as in this instance.

More than a century before Pope, William Shakespeare used the expression "I'll not budge an inch." Is Shakespeare here being guilty of the very offense that Pope objected to: the use of a shopworn expression? While it is true that "budge an inch" has been overused and become a **cliché**, it was fresh and new when Shakespeare coined it. Many of his brightest creations have become clichés because of overuse. Cliché has a negative connotation, but in its first use, the now overworked expression might have seemed good—so good that speakers copied it again and again.

The word *cliché* comes from a French word to *stereotype*. A stereotype repeats a pattern over and over. While it is true that one person's cliché may be another's little masterpiece, certain expressions have become so hackneyed that most speakers and writers avoid them in careful communication. The greater a person's sophistication, the greater the sensitivity to clichés.

Yet we can't all be careful and brilliant all the time. Clichés may often be substituted for thought, but sometimes they are helpful in establishing a bond for communication.

In making a case for the inevitability of clichés, Hugh Ranks says, "We need repetition and regularity for both clarity and speed. The more uncommon the word or phrase, the longer it takes for us to understand it. In our brain's memory bank, the search process takes longer, and we often get distracted from the flow of the conversation if we're searching out individual words. If all our messages were original, fresh, new and unusual, they would be hard for most of us to understand. Certainly, it would slow down communication to a snail's pace.

"We need such low-stress choices and decisions for most of our run-of-the-mill, trivial, and commonplace matters to conserve time, psychic energy, and effort for the really difficult, the uncommon, the atypical."

In writing, however, when the writer has time to think, minimizing the use of clichés like these is probably desirable: *teeth like pearls, dead as a doornail, fresh as a daisy, white as a sheet, brink of disaster, window of opportunity, road to oblivion, last resort.*

The following paragraph provides overkill, containing more than twenty clichés:

> *A prominent citizen, eminently successful in his line of work, rose to speak. "Gentlemen," he began, "unaccustomed as I am to public speaking, I must take this opportunity upon this festive occasion to say that I have taken a new lease on life. As luck would have it, though I once lay at death's door, I am now alive and kicking. It is my cherished belief that half the battle was won when I decided to join your happy throng. Rumor hath it that this club is better than medicine. I, at any rate, can safely say I gave the club the acid test and found it all to be good. I have had ample opportunity to see others, who are beneath contempt, come to grief through failure to realize one simple truth: that groups like this fill a long-felt want. Be that as it may, and to make a long story short, it does my heart good to be here, for this is the happiest moment of my life."*

There is a time for a cliché. The context is the key.

Climax

MACBETH: *Thou art the best o' th' cutthroats:*
Yet he's good that did the like for
Fleance: if thou didst it thou art the
nonparell.
MURDER: *Most royal sir, Fleance is 'scaped.*
—William Shakespeare

Up to this moment in *Macbeth*, events have been going Macbeth's way. He has attained the crown. The pretender to the throne, Malcolm, has fled into exile. Everything beneficial prophesied by the Three Witches for Macbeth has come true. Never secure, however, Macbeth sends murderers to kill Banquo and his son Fleance. Banquo, prophesied to be the father of kings, seems to be a real threat. Banquo is killed, but his son Fleance, also the father of kings, has escaped. This is a turning point, a **climax**. Macbeth's fortunes have changed suddenly. Climax has the Greek root, *ladder*, suggesting that the action has been climbing to this crucial point.

Climax has other meanings in different contexts, but in the play, climax refers to that point in which the resolution may be sensed. It may be compared to climbing a mountain, reaching the peak, and then looking down the other side.

The words *dramatic structure* may be applied to the study of many plays, especially the tragedies of Aeschylus, Sophocles, and Euripides, as well as those of Shakespeare. Such a play begins with the introduction, in which the stage is set for the events that follow. Complications and conflicts arise in the section sometimes called *rising action*. The climax is the turning point. The remaining sections play out the implications suggested by the climax. This section is sometimes called *falling action*. It is usually a smaller section. Then comes the *denouement*, also called *resolution* or *catastrophe*. The threads are tied together, and the anticipated conclusion is played out.

Determining the climax is a literary exercise, with occasional disagreements. Is Hamlet's failure to kill Claudius at prayer or his actual killing of Polonius in the Queen's bedroom the climax? A case can be made for either.

Crisis is used for moments of tension making the resolution inevitable. The play scene in *Hamlet* provides a crisis leading to the climax and resolution.

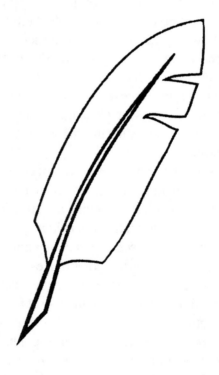

Codes and Ciphers

```
5 3 ‡ ‡ † 3 0 5 ) ) 6 * ; 4 8 2 6 ) 4 ‡ .
) 4 ‡ ) ; 8 0 6 * ; 4 8 † 8 ¶ 6 0 ) ) 8 5
; I ‡ ( ; : ‡ * 8 † 8 3 ( 8 8 ) 5 * † ; 4 6
( ; 8 8 * 9 6 * ? ; 8 ) * ‡ ( ; 4 8 5 ) ; 5
* † 2 : * ‡ ( ; 4 9 5 6 * 2 ( 5 * - 4 ) 8 ¶
8 * ; 4 0 6 9 2 8 5 ) ; ) 6 † 8 ) 4 ‡ ‡ ; ¶I
( ‡ 9 ; 4 8 0 8 I ; 8 : 8 ‡ I ; 4 8 † 8 5
; 4 ) 4 8 5 † 5 2 8 8 0 6 * 8 I ( ‡ 9 ; 4 8
; ( 8 8 ; 4 ( ‡ ? 3 4 ; 4 8 ) 4 ‡ ; I 6 I
; : I 8 8 ; ‡ ? ;
```

— Edgar Allan Poe

In "The Gold Bug," Edgar Allan Poe introduces an ingenious cipher. Though at first apparently unintelligible, it is solved step by step. Those steps provide an introduction to solving ciphers, an activity popular as a pastime and crucial in wartime.

Cryptograph is the general word for *secret writing*. Cryptanalysis is used in solving the secret writing.

Cryptography, the preparation of secret messages, may be divided into two groups: **ciphers** and **codes**. Ciphers ordinarily substitute symbols or letters to stand for letters in a message. Transposition of letter may be used as well as substitution. Codes usually depend upon prearranged substitutions. Sometimes a code book may be used. In a larger sense a dictionary is a kind of code book. If you have a word, you may look it up in the dictionary for its meaning. So for a code book. If the code book falls into the wrong hands, its secrecy is compromised.

The use of secret messages goes far back in history. Famous historical figures who have used ciphers include Julius Caesar, Charlemagne, Alfred the Great, Louis IV of France and Mary, Queen of Scots.

Mary's trust in ciphers cost her her life. In the dangerous world of Elizabethan Engand, plots and counterplots were frequent.

Elizabeth had become Queen after the turbulent reign of her half sister Mary Tudor and faced intrigues and possible insurrections. Mary, Queen of Scots, was a continuing source of worry. Both Elizabeth and Mary had descended from the first Tudor king, Henry VII. Mary had supporters who plotted to put Elizabeth to death and put Mary on the throne of England.

Fleeing intrigue in the Scottish court, Mary imprudently fled to England for protection. Upon the advice of her counselors, Elizabeth had Mary confined in a series of lodgings. Though treated well, Mary grew restive at the loss of her freedom and was tempted to listen to treasonous offers from outside supporters. She communicated in cipher with her English agents abroad, but the messages were intercepted and deciphered by Sir Francis Walsingham, English courtier. When informed of the treasonous interchanges, Elizabeth reluctantly agreed to Mary's execution. The cipher had given Mary a false sense of security.

Secret communication of all kinds is still a major concern of governments. Breaking the Japanese and German encrypted messages during World War II provided the Allies with a tremendous advantage. Conversely the Americans had a code that has been considered unbreakable. The Navajo "code talkers," as they were called, were able to transmit messages that the best enemy cryptographers were unable to decipher. They probably could have used just the Navajo language to befuddle the enemy, but in addition the code talkers devised a special coded alphabet. On top of all this complexity, the Navajos substituted clan names for military units, bird names for airplanes, and fish for ships. These three levels of mystification made Allied communications secure on those island-hopping campaigns in the Pacific.

Perhaps the best introduction to codes and ciphers is a book written just before World War II: *Secret and Urgent- the Story of Codes and Ciphers*, by Fletcher Pratt. It is fascinating, compelling, addictive. It reads like a good detective story.

Connotation-Denotation

"Clapped into a lunatic asylum, poor girl,"
said Mrs. Rhymer. A chill ran down her spine.
—Agatha Christie

In "The Case of the Rich Woman," Agatha Christie tells the story of a wealthy woman who relearns what is most important in life. Her outdated use of the phrase *lunatic asylum* strikes a negative note for most modern readers. In a time of more enlightened understanding, the expression is politically incorrect. More acceptable today might be *mental hospital* or another neutral-sounding label. *Lunatic asylum* and *mental hospital* have similar denotations but their connotations are far apart.

Denotation is the limited, literal meaning of a word. **Connotation** is the suggested meaning of a word apart from its literal meaning. *Lunatic asylum* and *mental hospital* refer to the same kind of institution, but the associations are quite different.

Childhood words are rich in connotation. *Mother* and *mommy* refer to the same person, but the connotations are dissimilar. "I called my mommy" has a different flavor from "I called my mother."

Some connotations are broad and general. *Democracy* has a favorable connotation for most Americans. *Terrorism*, on the other hand, is a descriptive word, but it brings a shudder for most persons. The word *attitude* has changed in recent years. Once a generally neutral word, *attitude* has taken on a new, negative denotation. "Fred has an attitude" now suggests an unpleasant demeanor.

Some connotations are individual. For many persons, the word *snake* causes shudders and repulsion. To a herpetologist, the word is rich with pleasant associations. A connotation may be limited to a singe individual. Even the generally loved word *ice cream* might have unpleasant associations for someone who overindulged and became ill.

A dictionary deals with denotations. It would be impossible to suggest all possible connotations of any word. Sometimes a word's general connotations finally make it to the dictionary definitions (denotations). When the word *notorious* first appeared in writing in 1555, it meant *well known; commonly or generally known; forming a matter of common knowledge* (*Oxford English Dictionary*). Gradually the word took on unpleasant connotations, which were finally incorporated in the dictionary definitions. *Webster's New World Dictionary* still lists the neutral definition first: *well known, publicly discussed.*

English is filled with words that have incorporated connotation into the dictionary meanings. Some words go uphill. A *constable* was once the officer of a stable. A *marshal* was a horse-servant. Some words go downhill. A *boor* was originally just a farmer. A *knave* was just a boy. Some words become narrower in meaning: *meat* once meant any food as in the expression *meat and drink*. An apparition, once an unusual or unexpected sight, is now usually limited to ghostly figures. Generalization in language also changes meanings in time. *Sailing* once meant voyaging in a sailboat; now *sailing* is a general word, applied even to objects: "the kite went sailing off." A *journey* was once a trip of one day's duration, from the root word *jour-day*.

Connotation is responsible for the fact that no two synonyms are exactly alike, interchangeable in all situations. *Limp, flimsy, loose*, and *flabby* are synonyms, but the connotations distinguish them. *Limp* may be applied to a straw figure, *flimsy* to a poorly built structure, *loose* to comfortable garments, and *flabby* to underused muscles. The denotation of weakness joins them, but their other meanings, influenced in one way or other by connotation, are quite different.

Those who wish to influence others use words rich in connotation. Political speakers employ prestige words like *integrity, loyalty, courage, unswerving devotion to duty*. Advertisers prefer *vitality, sparkle, glamour. Public relations counsel* sounds better than press agent. Even the lowly *prune* was renamed *dried plum* in an effort to improve its connotation.

A pitfall in attempting to converse in a foreign language is the user's unawareness of a foreign word's connotations. A language dictionary can go just so far. Language is magnificent, universal, and sometimes maddeningly individual.

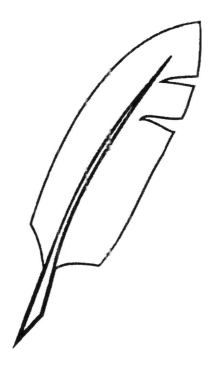

Context

"Ingmar Bergman's 'The Touch' Tells a Love Story Full of the Innuendos of His Genius."

According to this ad, I was the author of this cryptic and actually ambiguous paean, which was news to me.

—Vincent Canby

Movie critic Vincent Canby is complaining about the distortion of his review by the ad writer's editing part of the sentence out of context. A communication is meaningless unless it is set in a context stated or implied. The sentence in the ad was misleading because it was wrenched out of context implying a positive review when the review was mixed.

As usually defined, context is a weaving together of words, the words surrounding other words. Context may be nonverbal, too. Time, place, speaker- all provide different contexts that affect communication. "I'm a democrat" would have quite different meanings if spoken by an orator of ancient Athens, a resident of the "German Democratic Republic," in 1980 or a citizen of contemporary America.

Awareness of context is essential in reading editorials, columnists, or experts in any field. What context prompts a movie star to endorse a particular breakfast cereal?

Convention

Living room of the Chatfield country home, after dinner. Four women discovered sitting and talking.

—J.B. Priestley

This helpful information, at the beginning of the play *Dangerous Corner*, appears in the printed version of the play. When the play is staged, these directions become visual. The lines have been included here to emphasize the role of convention in art, especially drama. Simply put, **convention** is make-believe. A more informative definition has be offered by J.A. Cuddon:

In literature, a device, principle, procedure or form which is generally accepted and through which there is an agreement between the writer and his readers (or audience) which allows him various freedoms and restrictions.

The stage is a perfect illustration of convention. A room has only three walls. We are looking through the fourth wall. Part of a ship suggests the entire ship. If characters near each other are not supposed to see each other, we accept that convention. If stairs supposedly lead to an upper room we accept it, though we know the stairs lead backstage.

Time is a convention. Years pass. Characters age. New generations appear. The scenes change, from London to Paris to New York. At the beginning of *Henry V*, the Chorus exhorts the audience to imagine that the stage holds "the vasty fields of France," Two mighty monarchies are confined "within the girdle of these walls." We accept asides and soliloquies, although they are unrealistic to the unsympathetic critic. To enjoy the play, we develop a "willing suspension of disbelief."

Contemporary dramatists sometimes tweak convention. Two

living rooms appear on the stage, not side by side but overlapping. We accept the convention that when an actor is supposed to be in one living room, he or she doesn't see the furniture of the other living room. This spatial overlapping is somewhat like time overlapping. In another play, the same scene represents different evenings, different houses. We can tell by certain minor changes in décor.

Though convention is obvious in the drama, it functions throughout art. The conventions of traditional realistic representation were overturned by the impressionists, who looked at objects anew. Abstract Expressionism fostered still newer conventions.

In poetry, conventional diction was challenged in 1798 by Wordsworth and Coleridge. Modern-day poets challenge other conventions. The conventions of the traditional detective story have been challenged in a novel like *The Talented Mr. Ripley*, in which the principal character is a murderer.

A major appeal of convention is the desire of the reader or audience to be "in on" the deception. It's a kind of conspiracy, and we love it.

Couplet

Great wits are sure to madness near allied
And thin partitions do their bonds divide.
                                   —John Dryden

Couplets are lines of poetry rhyming in pairs. The first line rhymes with the second, the third with the fourth, and so on.

Couplets vary in length and in meter, as discussed elsewhere in this book. A couplet may have three poetic feet, as in Robert Browning's "Rabbi Ben Ezra."

Grow old along with me!
The best is yet to be.

The couplet may have four poetic feet, as in this verse from Jonathan Swift's satirical poem on his own death.

For poetry, he's past his prime,
He takes an hour to find a rhyme,
The fire is out, his wit decay'd,
His fancy sunk_ his muse a jade,
I'd have him throw away his pen,
But there's no talking to some men.

The couplet with five poetic feet is called the "heroic couplet." A list of poets who have used the heroic couplet includes some of the greatest names in English poetry from Chaucer onward. The quotation at the beginning of this entry is a heroic couplet.

Shakespeare often used the heroic couplet. Sometimes it marks the end of a scene or act, as in this couplet from *Hamlet*, which concludes Act V, scene 2.

An hour of quiet shortly shall we see,
Till then, in patience, our proceeding be.

Sometimes Shakespeare used couplets for the sheer joy of playing with words. He even broke up a couplet with two different speakers, as in this couplet from *Love's Labour's Lost*.

FORESTER. *Nothing but fair is that which you inherit.*
PRINCESS. *See, see, my beauty will be saved*
    by merit.

Love's Labour's Lost is unique in Shakespeare. Much of the play is written in heroic couplets.

Sometimes the couplet makes a sardonic commentary on the action. At the end of this same play, the King and his fellow suitors are to remain chaste for a year before they will have permission to woo the Princess and her maidens. The exchange between the King and Berowne, a courtier, suggests that the planned celibacy may not work!

KING. *Come, sir, it wants a twelvemonth, an'*
    a day, and then 'twill end.
BEROWNE. *That's too long for a play.*

This example takes even more liberties with the couplet, dividing the second line between two speakers. Again Shakespeare tests the "rules" and enjoys innovation.

Some couplets may have six poetic feet, but the heroic couplet is favored in poetry.

The couplet has gone out of style in modern poetry, but it is still alive and well in greeting-card verse. The compactness, the expected rhyme, the recognizable rhythm make the couplet a favorite element in many anniversary, birthday and holiday greetings. Amateur poets and lovers find the couplet an easy form to master.

Roses are red, violets are blue
Sugar is sweet, and so are you.

Poor poetry but maybe effective communication!

Deus ex Machina

JASON. *What can be strange or terrible after this? Two horrors: my dead sons, and the woman I will kill.*
(Jason batters at the doors. Medea appears above the roof, sitting in the chariot drawn by dragons, with the bodies of the two children beside her.)

—Euripides' *Medea*

The events in this brief quotation are the culmination of a long narrative. Many years earlier, Medea had aided Jason in his quest for the Golden Fleece, even murdering her brother Absyrtus in their flight from the enraged king of Colchis, her own father.

The two wanderers eventually come to Corinth, where they spend ten happy years together. During this period, Medea has borne Jason two sons. This idyll ends when Jason falls in love with Glauce, the daughter of King Creon. Medea pleads with Jason, but he is indifferent. She begins to fail physically and then plots revenge. She vows not to kill Jason but to doom him to a life of agonized regret. Through a trick she manages to kill Glauce and Creon. Then she murders her own sons as terrible punishment for Jason. In one translation, Medea declares, "My pain's a fair price to take away your smile."

Jason comes raging to confront her. The opening quotation demonstrates his rage and his cry for vengeance. Medea is in a hopeless spot. As Jason is poised to exact his revenge, an amazing event takes place. Medea disappears and reappears above in a chariot drawn by dragons. The sun god, Helios, has provided the means for her escape.

This device was a favorite of Euripides, though Sophocles and Aeschylus avoided it. Here, the unexpected arrival of the chariot saves Medea at the last moment. The problems of the plot have been solved by an event outside the chain of causality. The device has a name- **deus ex machina**- literally, "the god from the machine." In ancient drama, a device was actually used to lower deities onto the stage at a crucial moment in the plot.

The phrase appears in literary criticism today, usually as a negative comment. An unexpected and contrived resolution of the plot elements is called a "deus ex machina."

If a wealthy uncle, long supposed dead, suddenly reappears with the fortune needed to save the old homestead, that's a deus ex machina. Aristotle condemned this device, insisting that plot difficulties must be addressed without sudden, easy tricks.

The device is now more often used in comedy than in serious drama. However, if a lesser playwright finds himself at loose ends, with conflicting plot elements to be somehow resolved, he may be tempted to bring in that god from the machine.

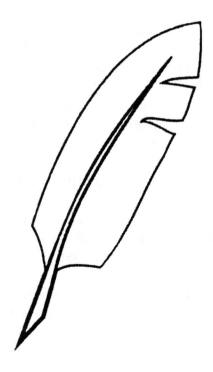

Doublespeak

*To everything there is a season, and a time to
be born and a time to die, a time to plant and
a time to pluck up that which is planted.*
                                        —Ecclesiastes

*A propitious, harmonious moment seems to
have been built into the very structure of
creation, with various options apparent as we
examine life, for the most part, with
perspicacity and comprehension, ever aware
of the contradictions inherent in even the
mundane activities of existence.*

What happened here? The second paragraph has taken the
Biblical simplicity of the first and turned it into a jumble of oversized
words that suck the blood out of the message. This is a good
example of doublespeak, the language, alas, of many politicians,
lawyers, educators, investment advisers, commentators, real estate
agents, and other practitioners of words.

Doublespeak, a branch of jargon, is characterized by
pretentiousness, complication, and obscurity. Doublespeak may
be intentional- to confuse, conceal, bewilder, impress. It may be
unintentional, a byproduct of uncertainty, confusion of thought,
and lack of writing skill. Doublespeak is easy to create. Choose
long, words of classical origin, cement them together with wordy
parenthetic expressions as for the most part above, and use five
words where one will do. Throw in as many abstractions as
possible

"It is required that all illumination, including the lights throughout
the room, be extinguished upon departing the premises."

Why not "Put out the lights when you leave?"

64

The first sentence has a kind of oratorical pseudoprofundity. The second sentence is brief, clear, forceful, with common words of Anglo-Saxon origin.

Of course, not every insight can be conveyed in concise Anglo-Saxon monosyllables. Some philosophical concepts require a greater complexity than "Put out the lights," but even such writing benefits from as much simplification and clarification as it will bear.

Some of our greatest patriots wrote well. Abraham Lincoln's *Gettysburg Address* is often used as a model of clear, concise language, emotional without being maudlin. Thomas Jefferson's the *Declaration of Independence* is clear and direct: "We hold these truths to be self-evident," not "It is apparent to all rational men that there are certain nonplatitudinous axioms that are clearly manifest." Though the sentences in these documents are long, they have no padding.

A more recent example of down-to-earth, simple, uncluttered speech is Harry S Truman's opening line of a campaign speech: "My name's Truman. I'm President of the United States, and I'm trying to keep my job."

Unfortunately, even common words can be strung together in overpowering detail. Absurd specificity can be overkill, as in this Interior Department regulation.

"No person hall prune, cut, carry away, pull up, dig, fell, bore, chop, saw, chip, pick, move, sever, climb, molest, take, break, deface, destroy, set fire to, burn, scorch, carve, paint, mark, or in any manner interfere with, tamper, mutilate, misuse, disturb or damage any tree shrub, plant, grass flower, or part thereof, nor shall any person permit any chemical, whether solid, fluid, or gaseous, to seep, drip, drain, or be emptied, sprayed, dusted or injected upon, about or into any tree, shrub, plant, grass, flower or part thereof…"

Why not "Don't disturb the plants?"

A troubling discovery: some contracts are drawn to be intentionally obscure and unreadable. Why? When contracts are overwhelming in detail and appearance, parties are less likely to attack the forbidding prose. When contracts are simplified and made more readable, clients then insist on reading every sentence, taking longer in the process, and even insisting on changes, often minute. Clarity is difficult at best. When its lack is part of the strategy, the consumer is the loser.

Someimes persons are impressed by unreadable prose. J. Scott Armstrong has written: "An unintelligible communication from a legitimate source in the recipient's area of expertise will increase the recipient's rating of the author's competence."

Alas, if you don't understand it, it must be good!

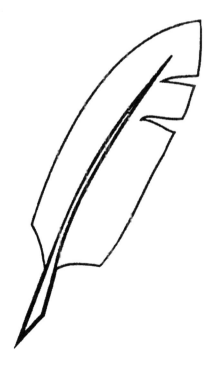

Doublet

*Fealty is used specifically of the feudal
obligation a vassal owed his lord. The oath of
fealty expressed both allegiance and fidelity.
Fidelity implies a strong and faithful
dedication. His fidelity to the principles of
justice never wavered.*

—S.I. Hayakawa
Modern Guide to Synonyms

Fealty and *fidelity* come from the same Latin root. English
often borrows the same root twice and provides a different meaning
for each borrowing. Such pairs are called **doublets**. *Royal*, from
the French, and *regal*, from Latin, are doublets both coming from
the root meaning *king*.

In its receptive attitude toward borrowing, English welcomes
new words, even if they have been recycled. The following doublets
show how varied are the sources of common doublets.

OLD ENGLISH AND LATIN eatable, edible; kin, genus
OLD ENGLISH AND FRENCH brother, friar; word, verb
OLD ENGLISH AND SCANDINAVIAN hale, hail; shriek, screech
OLD ENGLISH AND DUTCH eat, etch; slide, sled
FRENCH AND ITALIAN influence, influenza; study, studio
FRENCH AND SPANISH army, armada; musket, mosquito
GREEK AND FRENCH basis, base; papyrus, paper

Doublets may come from different periods of the same
language, like *carmine* and *crimson* from two different periods
of French. Doublets may come from two different dialects of a
language, like *cavalry* and chivalry from two French dialects. Or
doublets may result from various changes within English itself, like
history and *story*.

Some words appear in three, four, or five different forms.
Debit, *debt*, and *due* come from one root. *Gentle*, *genteel*,

gentile, and jaunty come form a single root, as do *discus*, *disk*, *dish*, *desk*, and *dais*.

Doublets are still being created.

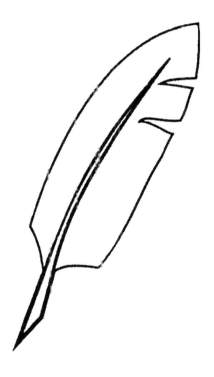

Elegy

I weep for Adonais- he is dead!
O, weep for Adonais! Though the tears
Thaw not the frost which binds so dear a head!
    —Percy Bysshe Shelley

These are the opening lines of "Adonais," a poem written by Shelley on the death of his young friend John Keats. It is a classic **elegy**, a lament for the dead, a tribute to the person's qualities and achievements.

Originally, the elegy had a less individual quality. It might be a general lament about the passing of time and the loss of those who have gone before. A section of "The Wanderer," an old English poem asks,

Where went the horse, the man, the treasure giver?
Where were there feast seats and the joys in hall?
Alas, the bright cup and the armored warrior,
Alas, the prince's glory! That day perished,
That bright time darkened under the helm of night,
And is no more.

This poem contains the "where are…" formula commenting on the ravages brought on by time. "Where are…the snows of yesteryear?" The same theme appears in literature from the days of Greece and Rome. Undoubtedly, some ancient poet by the waters of Babylon expressed a similar lament.

The perfect expression of the theme is found in "Elegy Written in a Country Churchyard" by eighteenth-century poet Thomas Gray. Many phrases from this work are quoted again and again. Some have been used for the titles of novels and plays, like "paths of glory" in the following stanza:

The boast of heraldry, the pomp of power,
And all that beauty, all that wealth e'er gave,
Awaits alike th' inevitable hour:
The paths of glory lead but to the grave.

A related word, **dirge** is shorter, less formal, and is intended to be sung. A **complaint** is a general term, expressing grief or dissatisfaction. **Eulogy** is sometimes confused with elegy. A eulogy expresses praise, without the element or sadness or grief. An elegy might contain a eulogy, but the two terms are quite distinct.

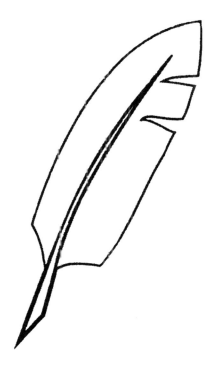

Epitaph

John Donne
Anne Donne
Undone

—John Donne

For terseness, this epitaph has few challengers. Though this is one of the shortest epitaphs on record, it is challenged by Dorothy Parker's flip comment:

Excuse my dust

As a famous actor, Richard Burbage had an even shorter farewell:

Exit Burbage

The etymology of epitaph suggests its meaning: *epi-* on: *taphos-* tomb. In *The Devil's Dictionary*, Ambrose Bierce, ever the sardonic commentator, defined epitaph in this way:

An inscription on a tomb showing that virtues acquired by death have a retroactive effect.

Epitaphs may be poignant, as Mark Twain shows in his epitaph for his daughter Susy:

Warm summer sun, shine kindly here,
Warm summer wind, blow softly;
Green sod above, lie light, lie light-
Good night, dear heart, good night, good night

Epitaphs may be revelatory, as in this epitaph attributed to the poet John Dryden:

Here lies my wife, here let her lie!
Now she's at rest, and so am I.

John Wilmot, Earl of Rochester, composed a mock epitaph for Charles II:

Here lies our Sovereign Lord, the King,
Whose word no man relies on.
He never said a foolish thing,
And never did a wise one

The King, who was very much alive at the time, had the rare privilege of commenting on his supposed epitaph:

My words are my own. My actions are those of
my ministers.

Thomas Hardy created a literary "Epitaph on a Pessimist."

I'm Smith of Stoke, aged sixty-odd,
I'd lived without a dame
From youth- time on; and would to God
My dad had done the same.

Robert Burns paid a subtle tribute to William Muir:

If there's another world, he lived in bliss;
If there is none, he made the best of this.

David McCord created the perfect epitaph for a waiter:

By and by,
God caught his eye.

Benjamin Franklin's famous epitaph used his printing career

for an extended metaphor:

> *The body of*
> *Benjamin Franklin, printer,*
> *(like the cover of an old book,*
> *Its contents worn out,*
> *And stript of its lettering and gilding)*
> *Lies here, food for worms!*
> *Yet the work itself shall not be lost,*
> *Yet it will, as he believed, appear once more*
> *In a new*
> *And more beautiful edition*
> *Corrected and amended*
> *By its author!*

John Gay had the most sardonic last word:

> *Life is a jest and all things show it:*
> *I thought so once, but now I know it.*

Epithet

Gray-eyed Athena sent them a favorable Breeze, a fresh west wind, singing over the wine-dark sea.

—Homer

In the *Odyssey*, the goddess Athena, partisan of Odysseus, has just sent the homeward-bound voyagers a favorable wind. Odysseus's enemy, the god Poseidon, provides other, contrary influences in the course of the voyage. This brief selection is noteworthy for two of Homer's most famous epithets: *gray-eyed Athena* and *wine-dark sea*. These adjective-noun combinations appear throughout both the *Odyssey* and the *Iliad*. They provide a satisfying shock of recognition.

Additional commonplace epithets in Homer include *swift-footed Achilles*, *cloud-gathering Zeus*, *godlike Paris*, and *white-armed Hera*.

A broader meaning of **epithet** is an adjective or phrase combined with a noun suggesting a quality or characteristic of a person or object: *Richard the Lionheart, murmuring brook, Honest Abe, Long John, Painted Desert*.

As so often happens, the world *epithet* sometimes slides downhill in meaning. If we hear, "Sam used some choice epithets," we suspect that the language was negative.

Eponym

A surefire way to become an eponym is to found a religion or religious sect. You do not have to be a Jesus, Brahms, Zoroaster, Buddha, or Mahomet. Many a lesser- Luther, Calvin, Wesley, Menno, Simons, Campbell, Swedenborg- has been eponymized.
—Willard R. Espy

An **eponym** is someone after whom a country or institution is named, whose name is closely associated with a movement or theory, or whose name is associated with a familiar activity or characteristic.

Eponyms are prolific word-generators. Horticulture alone accounts for many names: *gardenia* from Alexander Garden, *zinnia* from Johann G. Zinn, *wisteria* from Casper Wistar. Literature has given us *Falstaffian* from Falstaff, *quixotic* from Don Quixote, and *pander* from Shakespeare's Pandarus. Mythology has provided *mercurial* from Mercury, *martial* from Mars, *jovial* from Jove. Historical figures have supplied *sandwich* from the Earl of Sandwich, *sideburns* from General Burnside, *boycott,* Charles Boycott. Places have provided *bedlam* from Bethlehem hospital, *china, turkey*. Products and processes have provided *daguerreotype* from J.M. Daguerre, *watt* from James Watt, *graham cracker* from Sylvester Graham.

The adjective *eponymous* is applied to a character who gives his or her name to the title of a work: *Macbeth, David Copperfield, Silas Marner*.

Study of *eponyms* turns up some amusing stories. The flower name *Sweet William* is said to have been named by the English to honor their sovereign King William III. The Scots were not enamored of William, especially after the Battle of Killiecrankie. The name *Sweet William* stuck in their throats. They named the same flower *Stinky Billy*!

E-Prime

The little word is *has its tragedies. It names and identifies different things with the greatest innocence; and yet no two things are ever identical, and if therein lies the charm of wedding them and calling them* one, *therein, too, lies the danger.*

—George Santayana

Is infects language so deviously that while Santayana is deploring the dangers of the linking verb, he uses an example himself: "are ever identical." Note that the word *is* in "is deploring" functions as a helping verb, not a linking verb.

Is can cause problems. It makes statements that can cause misunderstandings, start fights, and destroy friendships.

The problem with *is* lies in its chameleon nature. *Is* performs many functions.

"Ted is my brother." (Is *of identity*)
"Ted is conceited." (Opinion)

The preceding sentences have the same structure, but they differ semantically.

"The room is 64 square feet." (Measurement)
"The room is untidy." (Opinion)

We can check the first statement with a ruler, but no measuring device can check the second. Those who understand that difference have taken the first step toward language sophistication.

C. David Bourland took a more drastic step. He decided to eliminate all forms of the *is* word in his own writing. He developed a system called **E-Prime**. Writing in this mode requires discipline and refinement of thinking. Note these examples:

"The ant is an excellent preacher because she is not talkative."
"None teaches better than the ant, and she says nothing."

The second sentence above is written in E-Prime. It has more direct thrust.

Linguists disagree about the value of E-Prime. Eliminating the linking verb altogether sometimes produces strained prose. Losing the *is* of identity, for example, may inhibit conversation. On the other hand, trying consciously to avoid or limit *is* and all its relatives sharpens thinking and develops awareness about the way *is* can make glib assertions masquerading as truth.

Inconvenience dooms the complete victory of E-Prime. We have been conditioned since birth in the glorious freedom that *is* provides us.

"This is my toy, not Laura's."
What child will say, "This toy belongs to me?"

"Mommy, Rex chewed up the rug. He's a bad dog."
Shall we have the child revise?
"Rex has manifested all the qualities of a bad dog."

This intentionally ludicrous pairing points up the universal use of linking verbs from childhood on.

Is and friends will probably never disappear from speech, but occasionally trying to write in E-Prime "is" an eye-opening experience.

It shows how flabby our thinking can become if we rely on *is* excessively.

Except for quoted examples, this entry has been written entirely in E-Prime. Did you notice?

Etymology

A panting syllable through time and space,
Start it at home, and hunt it in the dark,
To Gaul, to Greece, and into Noah's Ark
                                    —William Cowper

"The game is afoot."

Sherlock Holme's comment to his friend Watson may be applied to **etymologists**, philologists who delight in tracking down word origins. Word derivations in the dictionary are usually traced back as far as the classical period, Latin and Greek, but word sleuths go back even farther, often to the roots in ancient Indo-European.

The more intensive search sometimes provides unexpected results. From the ancient Indo-European word for *throw*, for example, we have *ballistics, embolism, hyperbole, diabolical, devil, parabola, parley,* and *parliament.* To be sure, these words have come a long way from their early beginnings. As civilizations and sophistication advance, greater subtleties are evidenced by the words, often used in metaphorical senses. The original Indo-European roots, 2000 of which that have been identified, tend to be concrete: *drive, burn, grow, bend, deep.* Abstract ideas come later with civilization.

The search may reveal living conditions experienced by our remote ancestors. The Old English word *bed* can be traced back to Indo-European *bhedh*: to bury, dig. The association suggests that the early beds were on the ground. The word *fossil* is an appropriate descendant of the same root.

Euphemism

By brooks too broad for leaping
The lightfoot boys are laid;
The rose-lipt girls are sleeping
In fields where roses fade.

—A.E. Housman

Though this is a verse about death, the poet has softened the message with meditative melancholy. *Sleeping*, especially, is an example of **euphemism**, a device of saying something disagreeable in pleasant or indirect words. The harsh reality of death has generated dozens of euphemisms: some humorous like *kick the bucket* or more gentle, like *pass away*. Insurance salespersons avoid the expression "When you die." Instead, they say, "If there is a claim." Once a *burial ground*, a cemetery has been called a *memory garden*.

Euphemisms often satisfy a basic human need. In ancient times navigation was a dangerous occupation at best. When the seas were stormy, vessels were tossed about and lost. One body of water that sailors hated to sail upon was the sea we now call *The Black Sea*. In those days, however, it had another name—*Pontus Euxeinus*, or "Sea that is hospitable to strangers." What prompted the sailors to call a sea they hated by such a flowery name? It was an impulse as old as mankind: to avoid putting the unpleasant into words, and perhaps even encouraging the unpleasant to become more pleasant. It was the same impulse that caused Eric the Red to call his ice-capped island *Greenland*, that caused more modern navigators to change *Stormy Cape* to *The Cape of Good Hope*.

Though euphemisms may perform a service by softening a blow, too many interfere with communication. Occupations may be concealed or distorted by euphemisms: *landscape engineer* for *gardener, tonsorial artist* for *barber, collection correspondent* for *bill collector, public relations counsel* for *press agent, house of detention* for *jail*.

Advertisers are especially prone to coin euphemisms. A broken-down house is a *handyman's special*. A used car is *reconditioned, reprocessed,* or *pre-owned*. A free offer comes with strings attached.

The motto K.I.S.S. applies to writing: "Keep it simple, stupid." Euphemisms sometimes provide the elegant form, where simple is better: *retire* for *go to bed, repast* for *meal, surplused* or *downsized* for *fired, uncontrolled altercation* for *riot, facilitate* for *ease, utilize* for *use, implement* for *do, state* for *say, similitude* for *likeness*.

The alert listener recognizes euphemisms, understands the part they play in communication, and chooses prudently. In formal writing, use euphemisms sparingly.

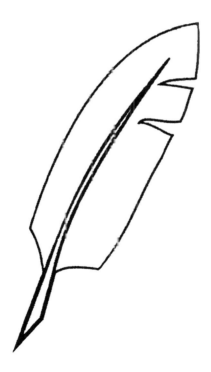

Fictions

The so-called riddles of the universe can never be solved, because most of what appears puzzling to us consists in contradictions created by ourselves, and arises from trifling with the mere shells and forms of knowledge.
—Hans Vaihinger

In *The Philosophy of As If*, Hans Vaihinger, nearly a century ago, provided insight into the ways in which we try to come to grips with a reality that is ultimately unknowable. We develop strategies, **fictions**, that help us function in the real world that is beyond our senses. Since we cannot pierce the veil, we act *as if* we can. We use language that is trickier than we realized. We develop elaborate philosophical systems that are ultimately closed systems—words about words, not one to one with reality.

Some fictions are obvious. The island of Malta was classified as a battleship by the British. Lines of longitude are latitude are fictions to help in navigation. Country borders are fictions of particular times. The borders of Alsace-Lorraine were oft-changing fictions: from France to Germany to France to Germany to France. The French Embassy in Washington is considered a part of France. We know that the Embassy is really geographically part of the United States, but we accept the fiction. Some fictions are not obvious.

Law is especially dependant upon fictions. It's a constant battle between slippery, ever-changing reality and inflexible words. Where necessary, the words eventually give way, but they are usually behind the events. By the time they have changed, reality has changed even more. If reality is like a writhing snake, law tries to tie it down before it wriggles again. But every snake is different. Every case is different, even though we presume that we can fit a case into a convenient box—a box created for us by preceding cases. The very word *case* suggests *box*, but boxes cannot confine reality. Every Supreme Court is different from its predecessors. Judges change. Contexts change. The law is what they say it is…at the time.

When Hamlet says, "There is nothing either good or bad, but thinking makes it so," he is not being an amoral, nihilistic philosopher ready to junk all standards. His comment shows an awareness of the conventional nature of human judgment. We have been culturally conditioned to see and feel in certain ways. We have our own idiosyncrasies that inevitably operate to affect our judgment. What we come up with is individual, but the relationship to the world outside us is fluid, uncertain, quixotic.

Vaihinger also has written, "The object of the world of ideas as a whole is not the portrayal of reality- this would be an utterly impossible task—but rather to provide us with an instrument for finding our way about more easily in the world."

All in all, these fictions work out reasonably well, so well at rimes that we mistake our world of words for the impenetrable reality around us and within us.

Entries in the book dealing with the fictions we create include *Ambiguity*, *Classification*, *Doublespeak*, *Paradox*, and *Symbols*.

Figurative Language

Born of the sun they traveled a short while
towards the sun,
And left the vivid air signed with their honor.
—Stephen Spender

How might this be expressed in other words?

Some individuals stood apart from their fellows
and left a mark.

What has happened here? What became of that glorious image of great individuals "who wore at their hearts the fire's center?" The first version contains magnificent **figurative language**. The second is colorlessly literal. There is a place for both, but recognizing the differences can enrich our own communication.

Figurative language is a kind of amiable deception. In figurative language, "it is what it isn't." It says one thing and means another. It adds color, variety, and sparkle to language. A strictly literal language would be dull.

Figurative language is not mysterious, exotic, reserved for poets and literary types. It is universal, everywhere, common in the language of a six-year-old and of an octogenarian. It is difficult to speak or form sentences without using some form of figurative language- usually metaphor.

Slang, that often misunderstood and underappreciated form of expression, is rife with figurative language. Slang's major weakness is its transience: eruption and then disappearance. But it is colorful, often sneakily insightful. Some slang words have become indispensable and even respectable, words like *highbrow*, *troubleshooter*, *wisecrack*, and *washout*. These words are figurative. Two major divisions of figurative language are **comparisons** and **associations**. Comparisons include *simile*, *metaphor*, and *personification*. Associations include *metonymy* and *synecdoche*. The expression **figures of speech** is sometimes used for figurative language.

Sometimes figurative language is combined with literal language in error. At other times the mixture is an intentional commentary, sometimes pungent and wry: "A neurotic builds castles in air. A psychotic lives in them."

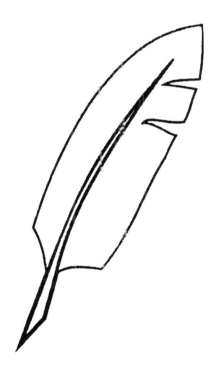

Foreshadowing

*Whenever these home supplies were
exhausted he would go to the Quiet Woman,
and standing with his back to the fire, grog in
hand, tell remarkable stories of how he had
lived seven years under the water-line of his
ship, and other naval wonders, to the natives,
who hoped too earnestly for a treat of ale from
the teller to exhibit any doubts of his truth.*

*He had been there this evening. 'I suppose
you have heard the Egdon news, Eustacia?'
he said, without looking up from the bottles.
'The men have been talking about it at the
Woman as if it were of national importance.'*

'I have heard none,' she said.

*'Young Clym Yeobright, as they call him,
is coming home next week to spend Christmas
with his mother. He is a fine fellow by this time,
it seems. I suppose you remember him?'*

'I never saw him in my life.'

*'Ah, true; he left before you came here. I
well remember him as a promising boy.'*

'Where has he been living all these years?'

*'In that rookery of pomp and vanity, Paris,
I believe.'*

—Thomas Hardy

In *The Return of the Native*, Thomas Hardy created one of
his most fascinating women. Eustacia Vye is headstrong, spoiled,
self-absorbed, passionate, dissatisfied, rebellious, but above all
beautiful and irresistible to men. She is "imprisond" on Egdon
Heath, a country backwater, dreary and dull for Eustacia. At the
moment quoted, Estacia's grandfather has offered the news that
Clym Yeobright, the native, is returning to Egdon Heath. Eustacia

sees this as an opportunity to flee her surroundings and join the colorful world outside.

Readers have been made aware of Eustacia's longings. The final sentence of the quotation suggests what is going to happen. Concise, understated, informative, it changes the thrust of the novel and puts Eustacia on the path that ultimately leads to tragedy.

This effective sentence is a superb example of **foreshadowing**, providing information suggesting future events. The reader's reaction might be called the "uh-oh response!" Reading about Paris and knowing too well what Eustacia is like- uh-oh!

Foreshadowing is common in all forms of literature. Shakespeare's plays use foreshadowing in the opening sequence: the ghostly battlements of Elsinore in *Hamlet*, the Three Witches in *Macbeth*, the opposing factions in *Romeo and Juliet*.

Foreshadowing may be complex. In Charles Dickens' *Great Expectations*, the hero, young Pip, is surprised by an escaped convict. Pip is moved to get Abel Magwitch, the convict, food and a file to break his chains. Though Magwitch is later captured, he vows to repay Pip. At first, the arrival of Magwitch foreshadows trouble for Pip, but when Magwitch promises to repay the boy later, Dickens is foreshadowing a very happy resolution.

Foreshadowing in detective stories is often intentionally deceptive. The guilt of a major character seems to be foreshadowed by the detective's incriminating discoveries, but the trails turn out to be false. If the guilty person's identity is a surprise, the author has succeeded.

The movies use foreshadowing. Certain stereotyped devices warn the audience that complications will ensue: the mysterious stranger at the wedding, the important-looking letter that arrives just after the protagonist has left the house, the young woman's bravado in going down alone into a dark cellar with a lighted candle.

By preparing for later events, foreshadowing may give unity to a novel, play, or film.

Formal Truths-Factual Truths

Liberty is the only thing you cannot have unless
you are willing to give it to others.
—William Allen White

This is a statement of truth, but it is a particular kind of truth—a **formal truth**. Both formal truths and **factual truths** hobnob together, but there is a considerable difference between them. The following are all formal truths:

A touchdown in football is worth six points.
The term of a senator is six years.
A singular noun is followed by a singular verb.

These are all true because people have agreed that they are true. All are subject to review. The three-point goal in basketball, for example, is a recent introduction, adding another formal truth. Formal truths are verbal truths. Legal precedents, though based on actual events, become formal truths, accepted by jurists and lawyers because they provide helpful guidelines in new cases. Though no two cases are exactly alike, lawyers try to find enough similarities to help their presentation.

Lighted gasoline vapor will explode.

This statement contains a different kind of truth. The rules of formal truths can be changed. People cannot agree to change the rules with this type of truth, a factual truth. Both types of truths are indispensable in our daily activities. It's important to know the difference.

Free Verse

When lilacs last in the dooryard bloom'd
And the great star early droop'd in the western
sky at night,
I mourned, and yet shall mourn with ever-
returning spring
—Walt Whitman

Whitman, considered one of America's greatest poets, here expresses shock at the death of Abraham Lincoln. Whitman suggests the time of the tragedy: lilacs blooming, spring. The drooping of the great star suggests the loss of Lincoln. The entire poem is a powerful tribute, a cry of great loss, but is it poetry?

Two common elements of poetry are lacking here: a formal metrical pattern and rhyme. Why didn't Whitman choose to accept the constraints of most poems and avoid the apparent looseness of his poetry? Instead he chose the liberation of free verse. Although it lacks a formal rhythm and rhyme, it has larger rhythmical units, best experienced when the verse is read aloud. It has a pulse, a cadence that can be felt but not regularized. Free verse encourages spontaneity, experimentation. If the unit of most poetry is the foot, the unit of free verse is the stanza.

Walt Whitman shocked America with the freedom of his verse and the range of his subject matter, but he was by no means the first practitioner. Hebrew verse and much Oriental poetry resemble our conception of free verse. The King James Bible uses free verse in the Psalms.

Free verse may look suspiciously like prose at times, and the dividing lines are slippery and subjective. A helpful mnemonic for discussing poetry is TIME: thought, imagery, music, emotion. Even in the brief excerpt quoted at the beginning of this chapter, Whitman's lines qualify as poetry. The four elements are broad enough to separate most prose from what we call poetry.

Poetry is not an absolute term. Are the following examples poetry?

1. Snow
        in the northern hills...
   Rain
        in the coastal valleys...
   Fog
        along the shores...
   Today.

2. How admirable:
   to see lightning and not think
     life is fleeting.

They are both arranged as free verse. The first is a weather report. The second is a famous haiku by the Japanese poet Basho. Who is to say that neither, one, or both are poetry? There is no final answer. Perhaps when an individual makes his own decision, that is enough.

Emily Dickinson's comment is interesting. "If I read a book and it makes my whole body so cold no fire can warm me, I know that is poetry." This may be too limited and restrictive, but it makes a point about certain types of lyric poetry.

Gender

In German, a young woman has no sex, while a turnip has. Think what overwrought reverence that shows for the turnip, and what callous disrespect for the girl.

—Mark Twain

Mark Twain is poking fun at one of the illogicalities of gender, especially as I appears in certain foreign languages. **Gender** is essentially a grammatical term, not the same as biological sex. In English there is no logical connection between gender and sex. *Stag*, *bull*, *ram*, and *stallion* link sex and masculine gender. *Doe*, *cow*, *ewe*, and *filly* link sex and feminine gender.

Some gender words are under attack. *Steward*, *actor*, and *chairman* are historically masculine in gender. Words like *stewardess*, *actress*, and *chairlady* are logically feminine in gender. There has been a strong tendency, however, to avoid what some people consider sexist labels. *Steward* and *stewardess* become *flight attendants*. *Actor* includes men and women. *Chair* replaces *chairman* and *chairlady*. Gender is inescapable with the singular of personal pronouns: *he*, *she*. The third pronoun, *it*, is considered neuter gender. Most nouns are of the neuter gender: *chair*, *house*, *notebook*. Some are of the common gender: *movie star*, *celebrity*, *pigeon*.

A pronoun should agree with its antecedent in gender as well as number (singular, plural).

"My brother does most of <u>his</u> car repairs. Dodie found <u>her</u> missing watch under a cushion. The car has lost <u>its</u> spare. A celebrity pays for <u>his</u> or <u>her</u> fame with anxiety."

Gender in English appears in certain conventional expressions, like *she* for boats. Some individuals refer to their cars, even a piece of machinery as feminine. "Watch that crane in operation. She's a beauty." Feminists don't always approve of these affectionate assignments of gender.

In many languages other than English, gender is an inescapable problem, often an illogical one. Because the article for example, is tied to the noun in these languages, users must know the gender—not the sex but the gender. Mark Twain is referring to the German word *Madchen*, girl. The article attached to it is *das*, thus classifying *Madchen* as neuter. *Weib* for wife is also neuter: *das Weib*! *Rube*, for turnip, is feminine and takes the feminine article: *die Rube*.

Inconsistency is rampant within languages, but linguistic comparisons reveal other oddities. A Spanish butterfly is feminine: *la mariposa*. But a French butterfly is masculine: *le papillon*. A German butterfly is also masculine, powerfully so: *der Schmetterling*!

The word *gender* is also used in sociological studies.

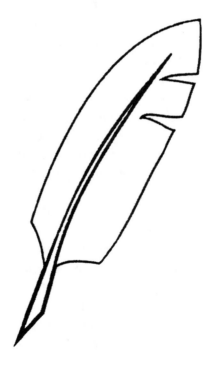

Gesture

> *"Master," cried the servant, "just now when I was in the marketplace I was jostled by a woman in the crowd and when I turned I saw it was Death that jostled me. She looked at me and made a threatening gesture."*
>
> *Terrified, the servant asked his master for a horse to escape Death. After the servant had ridden off to Samarra, the merchant became annoyed at losing the services of his servant. He went down to the marketplace to confront Death and complain.*
>
> *Death explained that the gesture was not a threat but rather an expression of surprise. "I was astonished to see him in Baghdad, for I had an appointment with him tonight in Samarra."*
>
> —Somerset Maugham

Gestures play a dramatic role in this fable about destiny. The misinterpretation of a gesture helped confirm the fate of the frightened servant.

Gestures complement other messages and sometimes have a message of their own. Gestures are more frequent in some countries than others; for example, Italy more than England. Gestures vary. In some countries, during a curtain call, actors wave toward themselves, accepting the applause of the audience. Actors in America smile and bow. As suggested in the entry for "Kinesics," an apparently inoffensive gesture may seem insulting in another culture.

As a form of body language, kinesics is usually concerned with involuntary messages. Gestures are usually controlled and intentional.

Grammar

The first thing you should attend to is to speak whatever language you do speak in its greatest purity, and according to the rules of grammar: for we must never offend against grammar.

—Lord Chesterfield

Grammar is a two-pronged word; the actual structure of a language and the study of that structure: how words are put together to make sense. The second meaning is the more common understanding. Grammar in the first sense is a concern of this entry.

The grammar of a language evolves over time. Vocabulary words come and go. Many new words are obsolete within a generation. Many of the words in Chaucer's time have disappeared. But grammar is more stable. If we can handle the language of Chaucer's *Canterbury Tales*, we feel fairly comfortable with the grammar.

Children learn the basic structure of English at an early age. They may say, "Me want cake" instead of "I want cake," but the parents soon teach the correct pronoun I. They soon learn types of sentences: "Can I go with Timmy?" They soon manage a compound sentence: "Jason took Sandra's doll, and she cried." It's not long before the young speakers add a complex sentence to the repertory: "When Larry goes to the movies, can I go, too?"

The ingredients are all in place at an early age. It is said that a young child knows more grammar than an educated foreigner attempting to grasp the intricacies of English. Even the uneducated person knows grammar and can make use of intelligible if faulty language. With maturity and sophistication come a greater flexibility and complexity of expression. Such achievement can be overdone, however. Sometimes the simpler expression is best, though not always possible.

Speakers of a language instantly recognize a language pattern, even if the vocabulary is difficult.

> *Ratiocination is a major weapon in the arsenal*
> *of the great fiction detectives.*

This is a difficult English sentence, but it is a sentence recognized as standard English by almost any speaker of English. Here's a simpler version of the same message.

> *Reasoning is an important skill used by*
> *fictional detectives.*

This simple sentence becomes gibberish if the structure is tampered with.

> *Detectives important en used is skill fictional by*
> *reasoning.*

Travelers to a foreign land bring dictionaries of the countries' languages to help them talk and understand. Some frustration is inevitable. Words by themselves do not provide satisfactory communication. The words must be arranged in a meaningful structure- grammar of the language.

Grammar is sometimes confused with usage. A sentence like the following is sometimes labeled "bad grammar."

> *I ain't a member of the Camera Club.*

In the strictest sense, this is an example of improper usage. The grammar, however, is unassailable: subject verb, predicate nominative. The word *ain't* presents the problem. *Ain't* is a potentially useful word. If used only as a contraction for *am not*, it would supply a missing word in English. *Isn't* and *aren't* are useful contractions for *is not* and *are not*, but we have no useful contraction for *am not*. Why not? For some reason, *ain't* ran afoul of society's arbiters and is now avoided in careful speech. Yet when the *are-not* contraction is called for in questions, the solutions don't sound right.

> *I'm invited, aren't I?*
> *I'm invited, am I not?*

The first seems precious. The second seems stuffy.

The word *ain't* goes back centuries. The *Oxford English Dictionary* has a citation from 1778. Usage can be arbitrary, even overruling the structure of language at times.

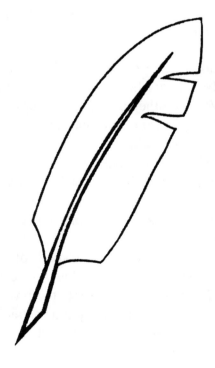

Greek Chorus

There goes Oedipus-
He was the man who was able
To answer the riddle proposed by the Sphinx.
Mighty Oedipus-
He was an object of envy
To all for his fortune and fame.
There goes Oedipus-
Now he is drowning in waves of dread and
*   despair.*
Look at Oedipus-
Proof that none of us mortals
Can truly be thought of as happy
Until he is granted deliverance from life,
Until he is dead
And must suffer no more.
                    —Sophocles' *Oedipus Tyrannus*

Here, the **Greek chorus** is commenting on the fate of Oedipus, who has blinded himself after discovering that he has married his own mother, Jocasta. . The familiar story is memorialized in the expression *Oedipus complex*. The conclusion to Sophocles' play demonstrates a function of the chorus in the plays of Aeschylus, Sophocles, and Euripides. It also gives us the phrase "Greek chorus," commented on below.

Chorus means *dance*. The chorus originated in dances performed in honor of the god Dionysus.

The early choral dances developed into drama, with first one, then two, later more than two speaking parts. In later plays, the chorus remained, though its importance diminished. The physical demands on the chorus are demonstrated in *Prometheus Bound*, by Aeschylus. As the chorus speaks, stage directions are included, like **strophe** and **antistrophe**. These words refer to the turns of the chorus as the members move about the stage.

The entry is relevant in the *Lexicon* because the phrase *Greek chorus* is sometimes applied to characters in plays or novels whose main function is to observe, to interpret, to comment about the actions of the other characters. In some detective stories, the narrator acts as a Greek chorus, commenting on the action without actively participating in it. We share the narrator's admiration at the detective's ingenuity. We now have been observers.

A representative example of the phrase *Greek chorus* appears in a recent review of *A Ladder in Hopewell*, a play about the kidnapping of Charles Lindbergh's son.

> *An ensemble of 11 actors play 20 roles as well as the chorus of reporters and local townspeople. This modern Greek chorus adds to the play a haunting and powerful mood.*

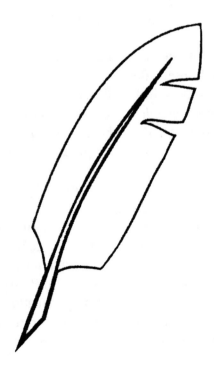

Haiku

Old dark sleepy pool...
Quick unexpected frog
Goes Plop! Watersplash.

—Basho

This is one of the most famous poems in the world. Why? What makes this unpretentious verse so significant? It is a perfect example of the **haiku**: a simple observation, devoid of philosophy, moralizing, or anxiety. In explaining Buddhism, R.H. Blyth states the point concisely: "The great problem of practical everyday life is thus to see things properly, not to valuate them in some hard and fast moral scale of virtue and vice, use and uselessness, but to take them without sentimental or intellectual prejudice." That immortal frog in the sleepy pool meets those requirements.

When Buddhism was exported to Japan, it took on a special flavor called Zen. The haiku is a terse expression of the philosophy of Zen.

In its original Japanese, the haiku is a seventeen-syllable verse form. Some translations try to use seventeen syllables. Others try to capture the spirit without the original number of syllables. No translation can hope to capture the full impact of the original. Indeed, there are many different translations of the frog haiku. But the haiku need not be enjoyed only in translation. English-speaking poets have tried their hand at original haiku.

A haiku is essentially a verbal snapshot, trapping a moment in time and sharing that fleeting impression for others' delight. The captured moment is important, not the poet.

Contemporary poets have attempted the haiku, a challenge that is deceptively simple. Two other frog haiku capture elusive moments.

Water striders make
The cloud reflections tremble.
Frog, join the dance
—Anne Filson

Rain drops from the roof,
Keeping time with the mantle clock.
Now, frogs, join in.
—Mary Holmes

The beauties of evening are often captured in haiku.

The full moon,
No leaf stirs. No owl hoots.
Even the cricket's voice is soft.
—Stewart W. Holmes

All is quiet now,
The night is like a heavy curtain.
The day's act is done.
—Priscilla George

The last, written by a high school student, suggests that haiku are worth attempting even by the reluctant writer.

The impulse to create a vivid objective image in words is not unique to the Japanese. R.H. Blyth has selected dozens of haiku-type examples from American and English literature.

The budding twigs
Spread out their leafy fan,
To catch the breezy air.
—William Wordsworth

The lark begins his flight,
And singing, startles the dull night
From his watch tower in the skies.
—John Milton

The lark at the break of day arising
From sullen earth
Sings hymns at heaven's gate.
—William Shakespeare

A young beech tree
On the edge of the forest
Stands still in the evening.
—Richard Aldington

Loveliest of trees,
The cherry now is hung with bloom
Along the bough.
—A.E. Housman

This brief selection deal principally with spring, always a favorite with haiku poets. Life is a succession of moments. The haiku selects one for sharing.

Homonym

Flattery is like soft soap; 90 percent lye.
—John S. Crosbie

In his encyclopedic *Dictionary of Puns*, Crosbie demonstrates that puns are alive and well. He often shows that puns depend upon similarity in sounds. *Lye* and *lie* are homonyms.

Homonym is a broad term, including the word *homophone*. Homophones are words that are pronounced alike but have different spellings and meanings: *right-write*. Homonyms in addition include words that are spelled and pronounced alike but have different meanings: *bear* (animal)- *bear* (carry).

Because of its many and diverse origins, English is especially rich in homonyms. Sometimes the homonyms derive from different branches of English. *Pale*, for example, has a Latin root; *pail*, a Middle English root. *Time* is from Old English; *thyme*, from the Greek.

A moment's reflection brings forth torrents of homonyms: *to*, *too*, *two*; *four*, *fore*; *dear*, *deer*; *sight*, *site*; *flower*, *flour*; *seize*, *sees*; *one-won*; *pore-pour*.

From the Greek, *homonym* means "the same name." **Heteronym** means "the other name." Words that are spelled alike but differ in meaning and pronunciation are called heteronyms: *lead-* (metal)-*lead* (guide); *bass-*(voice)- *bass* (fish); *row* (a line)-*row* (a fight).

Another word for heteronym is **homograph**—"same writing," but different pronunciation.

Humour

Come, he hath hid himself among these trees,
To be consorted with the humorous night.
Blind is his love, and best befits the dark.
                                        —William Shakespeare

In this passage, Romeo's friend Benvolio is commenting on Romeo's lovesickness. Modern readers of *Romeo and Juliet* are puzzled by the use of *humorous* here. Clearly, it doesn't mean *funny* in this passage, but this meaning of **humour** (the British spelling) here is an older one stretching back through the centuries. The current meaning, of course, is associated with comedy and fun. Everyone rejoices in the possession of a sense of humor.

The historical dictionary, the *Oxford English Dictionary*, traces the earliest uses of words and includes citations showing the meanings. The first entry in the *OED* for humor comes from the fourteenth century. Definitions *moisture* and *fluid* are close to the Latin root—*humor-moisture*. Words don't stand still. As the years pass, additional meanings are cited: *special bodily fluids*, like *blood*. This meaning is still the first in *Webster's Collegiate Dictionary, Tenth Edition*. The *American Heritage Dictionary* starts with the current meanings: "The quality of being laughable or comical funniness."

Medieval physiologists took the bodily-fluid idea further. They identified four chief humours: black bile, phlegm, blood, and yellow bile. A balance of all four is ideal, but what if one humour dominates? Then we have an unbalanced person at the mercy of his humour.

A person dominated by black bile, for example, will be *melancholy*. One dominated by phlegm will be *phlegmatic*; blood-*sanguine*; yellow bile-*choleric*. These adjectives may seem scientifically far-fetched, but we still use them today without any notion of how the words developed.

In 1598, Shakespeare's rival Ben Johnson, had a blockbuster

hit with his comedy *Everyman in His Humour*. The central concept was that each character was dominated by one of the humours. Legend has it that Shakespeare, himself, actually played a role in this play.

Those medieval physiologists also believed that there are four basic elements: air (cold), fire (hot), water (moist), and earth (dry). These elements were linked with the humours. Blood was hot and moist; yellow bile hot and dry; phlegm cold and moist; and black bile cold and dry.

People believed that humours may change over time. Observers noted that hot-blooded youths become less fiery. Thus in time a *sanguine* person may become melancholic. With the growing awareness of the role of body chemistry in health, perhaps the humours are partially returning under different names like *chemical deficiency*. The word *humour* is retained in medicine: *aqueous humor*.

In time the word *humour* was associated with a state of mind, an attitude, a mood. Those meanings remain in expressions like "Bert is out of humor today" or "Sheila is in a good humor." The verb *to humor* suggests adapting oneself to the whim or attitude of another.

Hyperbole

*I am, in point of fact a particularly haughty
and exclusive person, of pre-Adamite ancestral
descent...I can trace my ancestry back to a
protoplasmal primordial atomic globule.*
—W.S. Gilbert

When Pooh-Bah explains his ancestry in the Gilbert and Sullivan operetta The Mikado, he is indulging in a common literary and conversational device: **hyperbole**, exaggeration for effect. Our sense of the dramatic entices us to such expressions as *scared to death, frozen stiff, petrified with fear.* We may *cry our eyes out, hit the ceiling, explode in anger.* We may be *thunderstruck* when we get our tax bill, *paralyzed* when we see a tennis ball fly past.

The opposite of hyperbole is **understatement**. When Mark Twain wrote, "The report of my death is slightly exaggerated," he was using understatement for humorous effect. No one did it better. His essay, "Journalism in Tennessee," is a masterpiece of sustained, outrageous understatement.

English humor often relies on understatement. A major argument is a slight disagreement. An athletic victory *went fairly well.* A large inheritance is *a bit of money.* A severe injury is a *scratch.*

Like all linguistic devices that call attention to themselves, both hyperbole and understatement are effective when used sparingly and judiciously.

Icon

The Rolling Stones- gray, pale, bowed by the weight of three decades as pop icons- mount the mammoth stage.

—Marc Fisher

In describing a concert bathed in nostalgia, journalist Marc Fisher uses the word *icon* to suggest the idolatry lavished on the singing group for thirty years. From the Greek icon, "image," the word has had a long and fascinating history.

In the Eastern Orthodox Church, **icon** has a specific meaning: a pictorial representation of a holy figure: Jesus, saint, angel. The religious use has generated the word **iconoclast**, "image breaker," originally applied to an extreme religious group that destroyed the images as sacrilegious, idolatrous. **Iconoclasm** is an ongoing struggle between those who feel that religious art containing images of divinity encourages worship and those who see the depiction of holy personages as idolatrous. Islam forbids depiction of persons in religious art.

Icon broadened its meaning from the religious to the secular. A person who has achieved such fame and admiration to be loved may be called an icon, as in the opening quotation. In contemporary usage, a person who attacks comfortable beliefs and popular traditions is an *iconoclast*.

The word has become a household word with the introduction of the computer. An icon is a small image on the computer screen providing choices. As an example of resourceful use of an old word for a new concept, *icon* shows the flexibility of the English language.

Idiom

A candidate nowadays is a man who stands
for what he thinks the people will fall for.
                                        —*Princeton Tiger*

The simple sentence would be nonsense if translated into another language literally. *Stands for* and *fall for* are idioms whose total meanings are different from the sums of their parts. **Idiom** comes from a Greek root meaning "one's own." It denotes a word, phrase, or expression peculiar to a language with a meaning quite different from its logical or grammatical one.

Some years ago, nonnative speakers of English were amazed to see signs near LaGuardia airport. "Give the grass a break." Not familiar with the idiom, they read the sign literally and wondered at the invitation to destruction. The sign presented no problems to native speakers.

Equally puzzling to foreigners are expressions like these: "Stop bothering me. Cut it out!" or "Lay off!" or "Drop it!" or even "Go jump in the lake!" There are many other similar idiomatic expressions, all different in meaning from the meaning of the words as individuals. With idioms, one plus one doesn't equal two.

Many idiomatic expressions are familiar elements in everyday speech: *do or die*, *win or lose*, *spick and span*, *tried and true*, *far and above*, *neither here nor there*, *fine and dandy*, *all or nothing*. The list goes on, into the thousands. In learning a foreign language, a student must become familiar with the common idioms. These are learned by native speakers early. Because the expression are so common, they tend to be absorbed in childhood. Foreign students of a language have no such advantage, though of course they have absorbed the idioms in their native tongue.

An idiomatic expression is peculiar to a particular group, individual or style. Idiomatic English, for example, is subtly correct. It has the ring of truth, appropriateness, accuracy. It is devilishly difficult, even for a cultivated nonnative speaker, to speak or write idiomatically.

By a quirk of language, the word *idiot* comes from the same root as *idiom*. Words often have a tendency to go downhill. The word *idiotes* in Greek originally meant a private person, then a plebeian, a layman, and then an ignorant person. In disagreements, the word *idiot* has served as an unkind put-down. It has come into clinical disrepute for the retarded person.

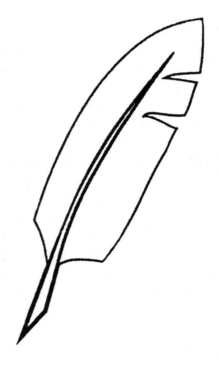

Imaginary Language

Some sample words: in Sindarin, the word for hobbit *is* periain *(pronounced peri-ain) and* is iron, duath *means* darkness; hir *means* hard. *In* Quenya, parma *means* book, anga *is* iron, heru *is* lord, lumbule *is* darkness.

—Jenny Price

Sindarin? Quenya? What's going on here? These are the two languages of Elves in J.R.R. Tolkien's *The Lord of the Rings*. For his literary purposes, Tolkien, created these two languages, clever and consistent. When the film *The Lord of the Rings-The Fellowship of the Ring* was produced, David Salo, an expert in Tolkien's **imaginary languages** was brought in as an advisor. The languages appear in the film with English subtitles.

Why did Tolkien bother? Why not use English in a way that the inhabitants of Oz or Alice's Wonderland do? Apparently, he enjoyed the challenge. The exotic words added a sense of mystery to the text. He had a respect for language and tried to create a grammar and vocabulary that sounded alien but also resembled living languages.

The impulse to create language is probably universal. Children make up secret words and languages to keep outsiders in the dark. Their languages use nonsense syllables in place of actual words, but they tend to retain the sentence structure of their native language.

In the search for a universal language, more than one hundred have been created. The most famous is Esperanto, devised in 1887 to break down barriers between countries by providing a common language. It has had energetic proponents and some limited success, but it has never taken hold universally.

English is the closest to a universal language. It has become the language of commerce and technical interchange. It is said that an Italian pilot approaching an Italian airport uses English for communication. Euro-English is planned, with phonetic changes introduced to overcome the difficult spelling of English. Before the dominance, a form of English was devised to become a universal language.

Basic English was devised by Ogden and Richards and presented in 1930. The vocabulary was limited to 830 words: 600 nouns and 150 adjectives. The remainder were "operators": verbs, adverbs, prepositions and conjunctions. Verbs and adverbs when combined can suggest a wide variety of meanings. *Call down*, for example, can replace *blame, criticize, denounce*, and several other synonyms. One problem is that these marvelous verb-adverb combinations are idioms, familiar only to native speakers of English, who don't need Basic English in concourse with each other.

Languages grow organically. Esperanto and others like it are created artificially, often with hooks to other languages. But that partial use of other languages is not enough.

In the appendix to his novel *1984*, George Orwell created an artificial language by transforming ordinary English. He called his creation "Newspeak," the language of a future in which the world is controlled by three dictatorial superpowers. "The purpose of Newspeak was not only to provide a medium of expression for a world-view and mental habits proper to the devotees of Ingsoc, but to make all other modes of thought impossible." It stifled the normal organic growth of a living language, reducing the number of words available for communication and strictly limiting those older words retained.

Here's an example. "The word *free* still existed in *Newspeak*, but it could be used only in such statements as 'This dog is free from lice' or 'This field is free from weeds.'" Old senses of political, economic, or intellectual freedom had been expunged from the language. The constant narrowing and extinction of connotations resulted in a rigidly controlled way of looking at the world. Looking at the world is made possible and comprehensible by the language we speak.

Hitler's Germany and Stalin's Russia developed a kind of Newspeak. Words meant what the Nazis wanted them to mean. "Freedom through labor" could greet victims slated for the gas chamber. Stalin's pawn, East Germany, called itself the *German Democratic Republic*- a corruption of the word *democratic*.

Orwell showed how distorting and narrowing word meanings could lead to tyranny. A living, unconstrained language is a defense against thought control. Artificial languages, as well as distorted living languages, demonstrate how languages can be manipulated for evil.

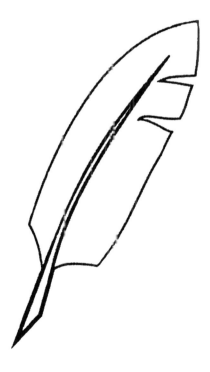

110

Indo-European

*In the mind of the average person language is
associated with writing and calls up a picture
of a printed page. From Latin or French as he
meets it in literature, he gets an impression of
something uniform and relatively fixed. He is
likely to forget that writing is only a
conventional device for recording sounds and
that language is primarily speech. Even more
important, he does not realize that the Latin
of Cicero or the French of Voltire is the product
of centuries of development and that language
as long as it lives and is in actual use is in a
constant state of change.*

—Albert C. Baugh

As long as human beings have engaged in social interaction,
they have used language. Neolithic tribes functioned successfully
using a speech we can only guess at. Michael Girsdansky suggests,
"All we can say with anything like certainty is that six or eight
thousand years ago there were men who spoke a common tongue
(or group of closely related dialects). And from that speech
descended the language spoken today by half the people of the
world," including English. They were speakers of the language
that scholars have labeled **Indo-European**.

That those tribes migrated seems likely, but from where to
where? Though the question may be unanswerable, clever
etymologists have made a good case for northern or north central
Europe rather than a more tropical locale. Those more tropic words
probably were added later.

As Mario Pei has pointed out, "Most of the branches hold in
common certain words for plants, animals, and minerals that exist
in north central Europe, but not other words denoting objects
existing on the Iranian plateau or in northern India. For example,

most of the early Indo-European languages show native developments of the same original root for *birch, beech, willow, ash, wolf, bear, goose, horse, dog, gold, silver*, but not for *palm, olive, vine, laurel, tiger, elephant, lion, leopard*."

No matter what the origin, the spread of Indo-European was phenomenal. Wandering bands lost touch with each other, and language differences emerged. Ten major groups formed. Two became extinct: the Hittite and the Tocharian- but the other eight are alive and well in the speech of their descendants. Those survivors comprise Indo-Iranian, Armenian, Greek, Balto-Slavic, Italic, Germanic, and Celtic. Those groups, too, splintered. Latin, a member of the Italic group, ceased to exist as a living language, but its influence lives on in modern English, as well as in the Romance languages of Europe.

For most purposes, tracing a word back to its classical ancestors is adequate. For example, tracing *magnify* back to two Latin roots meaning *great* and *make* is satisfactory, but the true etymologist doesn't stop there. He traces the word back to its Indo-European root, *meg(h)* meaning *big*, and he points out that a host of other words have descended from this one root; for example, *maharajah, megaphone, magnanimous, mayor, majestic, mister, maestro*. All eight surviving branches will have retained the root in one form or other.

The search is often fraught with difficulties. Sometimes the origin is obscure. The common word *pebble*, for example, can be traced back to Old English, where the trail grows cold. Sometimes the search stops before it begins. For the word *dodge*, dictionaries merely state, "Origin unknown." Sometimes authorities disagree on the etymologies. *Fix* is often supplied two derivations: a root for *fasten* and a root for *sharpen*.

We have been speaking of Indo-European languages. Important and widespread as they are, they do not embrace all the world's languages. In Europe, alone, several languages are often classified as non-Indo-European: Finnish, Estonian, Hungarian, and Lapp.

"Lost Languages" in this book suggests the diversity of languages and the threats to their survival. Many of these "other" languages have provided useful English words. Native-American languages, for example, have enriched English with a great many words. In foods alone, native speakers have provided not only the food but the corresponding words: *hominy*, *maize*, *pecan*, *succotash*, *squash*, *persimmon*.

Words enter English all the time. (See **Neologisms**) For an invented word like *pixel*, the etymology is brief. Some words, like *download* are combinations of existing elements. Brand names like *Microsoft* have become instantly recognizable. There is an exuberant proliferation of new words every year, some of them destined for a short life.

A final word. Sometimes native users create wholly new words by a process called "folk etymology." *Asparagus* is a somewhat forbidding term, so some speakers created *sparrow grass*, certainly a more poetic name! Cucumbers are sometimes called *cowcumbers*. *Bronchitis* becomes *brownkitis*. There is *no rabbit* in *Welsh rabbit*, *no buzz* in a *buzzard*. A *primrose* is not a *rose*, and a *barberry* hedge is not a *berry* hedge. *Cutlet* is derived from the word for *rib*, not *cut*. *Pantry* is related to the word for *bread*, not *pan*.

Studying word derivations is a rewarding hobby.

Inductive-Deductive Reasoning

When you have eliminated the impossible,
whatever remains, however improbable, must
be the truth.

—Arthur Conan Doyle

The great detective, Sherlock Holmes, is emphasizing one of his basic approaches to solving a case: observing, gathering information, and finally coming to a conclusion based on the evidence. Actual crime detection depends upon this procedure. This is the scientific method, the method of **induction**.

Inductive conclusions, because they are rooted in the real world, are subject to review, modification, and reversal. Many scientific theories in the past, derived from supposedly reliable instances, have been overturned when later evidence has been presented. In the real world, there is always the possibility of an actual event outside the carefully compiled statistics. We rely upon these scientific conclusions because we must. Certain medications work for 98% of the people, but those 2% just don't fit. Advertised panaceas for arthritis must also list the possible side effects, a medication not for everyone. Scientific generalizations are constantly under review—often by the researchers who promulgated them. Scientific conclusions are concerned with questions of fact and truth—slippery ingredients at times.

An inductive argument does not claim that its conclusions are absolutely true and certain. It claims merely that there is evidence for the truth of the conclusion. Inductive arguments are evaluated as probable or improbable. They are judged by questions like these:

1. How many experiences were considered?
2. Were these experience representative examples?
3. Were the experiences sufficiently similar?
4. Have times and conditions changed since the experiences were considered?

Sherlock Holmes's masterful conclusions based on the evidence he has observed are heady stuff. "How did he do it?" Unfortunately, in the real world, Sherlock mightn't have scored only bull's-eyes. It is impossible to assemble *all* the facts in every case. There's always the possibility that some unknown, unanticipated bombshell might destroy the case. The method in hands of reliable investigators works well...nearly all the time. But DNA evidence has freed many prisoners wrongfully accused on the accumulation of the best evidence *at the time*.

Inductive reasoning is wide open. **Deductive reasoning** is closed. Deductive reasoning is concerned with validity. It is best analyzed by looking at the syllogism, with its three parts,

Major premise: Little brothers are pests. (A is B)
Minor premise: Derek is my little brother. (C is A)
Conclusion: Derek is a pest. (C is B)

As an example of deductive reasoning, the syllogism is unassailable, the conclusion has been derived from the premises. The argument is valid. Problems arise when one of the premises is weak or the conclusion is improperly drawn from the premises. In the following premise, the major premise is unsound. The conclusion however is "sound," oops, valid.

All people below the poverty line use cocaine. (not true)
The defendant lives below the poverty line.
The defendant uses cocaine. (not true)

The minor premise may be unsound

All fish are cold-blooded.
Whales are fish. (not true)
Whales are cold-blooded. (not true)

As a deductive argument, the foregoing is valid, though absurd.

Another weakness in deductive reasoning is drawing conclusions improperly from the premises.

Public libraries are designed for the people.
This is a public library.
This library should be open 24 hours a day.

The premises are acceptable, but the conclusion is improperly drawn from the premises. An error in reasoning is called a **fallacy**.

It is possible to be an expert debater, trained in logic and the validity of conclusions. It is also possible at the same time to be ineffective, uninformed, or even deceitful. If the facts upon which the arguments are based are in error, all those beautiful syllogistic conclusions are worthless.

Sometimes the arguments are not presented in neat syllogistic form. An opinion, judgments, or conclusions may be stated with the premises implied. A statement like "eighteen-year-olds should be given the vote" implies premises like these:

All responsible citizens should be allowed to vote.
Eighteen-year-olds are responsible citizens.
Eighteen-year-olds should be allowed to vote.

Inclusive words like *all* are common in a syllogisms, but these are often misleading in the real world. Someone using the word *all* may be making a sweeping generalization that may not hold up in reality; for example, "All Dobermans are vicious." They are not. (Note that the qualifier *may not* prevents the statement from being itself a flawed generalization.)

Philosophies are closed systems. When the premises are accepted, the conclusions seem true. Hitler's evil philosophy was built upon the maligning of Jews.

All Jews are evil and should be exterminated.
Anne Frank is a Jew.
Anne Frank is evil and should be exterminated.

This is a monstrous conclusion, but it is perfectly valid if we accept the major premise.

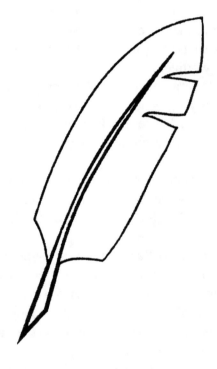

Inference

> "It's too bad," Colonel March went on
> sadly, "but the crime was from the first the
> work of a color-blind man. Now, none of the
> rest of you could qualify for that deficiency.
> As for Sir Rufus, I can think of nothing more
> improbable than a color-blind art collector-
> unless it is a color- blind interior decorator.
> Mr. Conyers, who shows by the blended hues
> of brown or blue in his suits, shirts, and ties
> that he has a fine eye for color effect; and he
> possesses no wife or valet to choose them for
> him."
>
> —Carter Dickson

At the end of *The Crime in Nobody's Room*, the fictional detective Colonel March is explaining how he solved the case. He has based the solution on the murderer's color-blindness. Along the way, March has drawn certain inferences. First, he eliminates the other possible suspects. Rufus is an art collector. Therefore he cannot be color-blind. Anita Bruce is an interior decorator. Therefore she cannot be color-blind. March skillfully demonstrates that all the innocent characters have excellent color discrimination. Then he proceeds to give instances in which the murderer has demonstrated color-blindness. A clever detective story provides all the clues, though some are slipped slyly into the narrative. March has come to his conclusion by drawing inferences.

Inferences are not confined to detective fiction and real-life crimes. People use inferences all the time.

The weather report predicts rain. I'll bring my umbrella.

A simple inference and a helpful one. Sometimes, though, the inference may be unwarranted.

Erin hasn't answered my letter. She wants to break off with me.

The inference drawn is only one of several possible inferences. The letter may have been lost in transit. Erin may be away an extended vacation. Erin has good intentions but a short memory. All are possible. To fasten upon only one may be unwise and unfair.

Inferences are always subject to correction. Even Colonel March may have expected too much of his ingenious inferences. In real life, perhaps the exonerated Mr. Conyers might be actually color-blind, counting upon someone other than a wife or valet to help him with his color coordination. Miss Marple, Ellery Queen, and other fictional detectives rarely draw a wrong inference. Actual detectives wish they were so lucky!

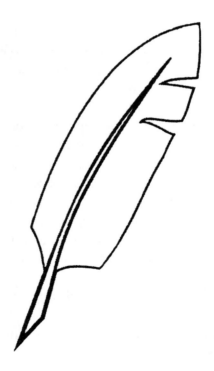

Inflection

I laid their daggers ready,
He could not miss 'em. Had he not resembled
My father as he slept, I had done 'it.
(Macbeth stands at the door, his bloody arms
indicating that he has killed King Duncan.)
My husband!

—William Shakespeare

At this crucial moment in *Macbeth*, just after Macbeth has done the deed, Lady Macbeth has two words that are open to at least a half dozen interpretations All are possible. Do the words suggest panic? Terror? Anxiety? Regret? Uncertainty? Questioning? Scorn? The chosen interpretation will be suggested by the inflection of her comment, the intonation of her voice, and the phrasing. Shakespeare lets the actor and the director decide on the rendering of this reaction.

Inflections are changes in pitch that effect the meaning of the spoken word. The written word is more open-ended. The written report of a conversation cannot capture the nuances of the spoken word. Indeed, written dialogue lacks another important element of communication: body language. *(See "Kinesics.")*

In the study of language, inflection has another, quite different meaning. An inflection is the change in the form of a word to show a grammatical function. In the word *trains*, -s is an inflection indicating that the word is plural. English has inflectional endings to indicate case, tense, plurality, gender, and other functions, but these inflections are relatively few when compared with those of German, for example. Contemporary European languages tend to be more highly inflected than English. Russian, for example, has subtleties of tense reflected in the physical form of the verb. Fortunately, the English language has dropped most inflectional endings, retaining only a relative few.

Languages that rely heavily upon inflections are called

synthetic. Those that rely principally upon word order are labeled **analytical**.

A comparison of a brief Latin sentence with a corresponding English sentences will show differences.

Latin- Puer amat puellam.
English- Boy loves girl.

Although the word order given for the Latin sentence is typical, the word order can actually be shifted without affecting the plain sense of the sentence: *Puellam amat puer*. Same boy loves same girl. The English word order cannot be changed in the same way without changing the meaning of the sentence: *Girl loves boy*. In Latin, the message is contained in the inflection: *puellam* is the objective case of *puella*, wherever it occurs. In the first English sentence, *girl* is in the objective case because of its location in the sentence, not because of any inflectional endings.

Language is not just inflections and word order. Linguists are discovering that languages outside the Indo-European group display surprising qualities and functions far different from our own. Mario Pei declares, "As for the simplicity of primitive languages, that is totally a figment of the imagination. In some Eskimo languages, a 'noun' can have more than one thousand forms, each with its own precise meaning. In a language of Guatemala, any verb can have thousands of different forms, by the addition of various endings. In the tongue of the Kwakiutl Indians, you cannot say 'the man lies ill,' but you must phrase it somewhat like this: 'This-visible-man-near-me, I-know, lies-ill-on-his-side-on-the-skins-in-the-present-house-near-us.'"

(See also "Syntax.")

Irony

O, beware, my lord, of jealousy;
It is the green-eyed monster, which doth mock
The meat it feeds on.

—William Shakespeare

When Iago warns Othello to beware of jealousy, the audience knows that Iago is the cause of Othello's jealousy. While pretending to be a dear friend of Othello, Iago is planning to destroy him. **Irony** may be defined as a *confrontation of opposites*. It is the awareness of what *is* and what *appears to be*. Iago appears to be concerned about Othello's jealousy. He really is the cause.

Irony may be **verbal** or **nonverbal**. In verbal irony a message implies something quite different from what is said, as in the Iago-Othello example. In nonverbal irony, a situation has implications far beyond the obvious. A man nearly dies of thirst a few yards from a hidden water hole. "How ironic," we say. The man's desperate situation is opposed to the salvation so close. The appearance is opposed to the reality.

Irony needs an observer to evaluate the contradiction, to set up categories which produce the contradictions. In *Othello*, jealousy and honesty are verbal classifications. Their disparity produces irony. One of the finest examples of irony is embodied in a simple quatrain by Sarah Norcliffe Cleghorn:

The golf links lie so near the mill
That almost every day
The laboring children can look out
And watch the men at play

This was a weapon against the exploitations of child labor.

Jargon

*The best actors in the world, either for
tragedy, comedy, history, pastoral, pastoral-
comical, historical-pastoral, tragical-
historical, tragical-comical-historical-
pastoral, scene individable, or poem unlimited.
Seneca cannot be too heavy nor Plautus too
light. For the law of writ and the liberty, these
are the only men.*
—William Shakespeare

Upon the arrival of the players at Elsinore in *Hamlet*, Polonius
shows off his knowledge of plays with this absurd catalogue of
play types. His list of words used in the theater illustrates one
definition of **jargon**: the special language of a group or profession.

Education journals are filled with words like, *coping
strategies, creative thinking, decision making, enrichment,
frame of reference, goal oriented, innovative, interpersonal,
meaningful, problem solving, pupil-centered,* and *resource
person.* Though sometimes a refuge from thinking, words like
these do provide easy communication for those in the profession.
Similarly, sports, television, medicine, the law, politics- all have a
specialized vocabulary sometimes necessarily technical.

There are other examples of jargon. A strange language,
gibberish, or nonsense may be labeled *jargon.* Another definition
is a failure to communicate effectively and economically.
Doublespeak has already been mentioned, with examples of
longer passages, but the corruption of language on a lesser scale
earns the *jargon* label, as well.

Pretentiousness, pomposity, and snobbery are enemies of
clarity in communication. One airline calls its flight attendants in-
flight customer-service representatives. The simple word *now*
is transformed into *currently, presently, at this point in time,* or
even as we speak. Active becomes *action-oriented.*

Economical becomes *price-oriented.*

Certain language habits suggest the wordiness of jargon. Introducing irrelevant words, even if not pretentious, interferes with communication. The intrusive *you know*, and *like*, and *okay* call attention to themselves and away from the message. "Being on that roller coaster, you know, was like exciting, but I was happy, you know, when the ride ended. Okay, I did go on again."

Pretentiousness, pomposity, and snobbery are enemies of clarity in communication.

Other names for jargon include *gobbledygook, officialess, legalese, bafflegab, cant, jabberwocky,* and *argot.*

An amusing wordplay with jargon is the humorous attempt to write as poorly as possible. The international Bulwer-Lytton fiction contest encourages contestants to submit amusingly bad entries: the opening sentence of the worst of all possible noels. The novelist Edward Bulwer-Lytton began *Paul Clifford* with the much parodied "It was a dark and stormy night."

In a recent contest, the winners were short:

> *Stanley looked quite bored and somewhat detached, but then penguins often do.*

And long:

> *The sun oozed over the horizon, shoved aside darkness, crept along the greensward, and, with sickly fingers, pushed through the castle window, revealing the pillaged princess, hand at throat, crown asunder, gaping in frenzied horror at the sated, sodden amphibian lying beside her, disbelieving the magnitude of the frog's deception, screaming madly, "You lied!"*

It's not easy to write that badly!

124

Jeremiad

Beloved brethren, know the truth: this
world is in haste, and nears its end; and so, in
the world, ever the later is the worse, and
because of men's sins it must needs from day
to day grow very evil e'er Antichrist shall
come; yea, truly, then will it be dreadful and
terrible all over the earth.

—Aelfric

Aelfric, a Benedictine monk who lived a thousand years ago, is noted for his prolific sermons and lives of the saints. The quotation records a sermon by Wulfstan, Archbishop of York. As the year 1000 approached, many envisaged the end of the world, as did Wulfstan. This quoted sermon may justly be called a **Jeremiad**, named after a major Hebrew prophet of the Old Testament. The book of Jeremiah contains a lengthy series of lamentations, calls to his fellows to mend their evil ways to avoid retribution. Though taking its name from a Biblical prophet, the word *jeremiad* has broadened to mean any prolonged lamentation or complaint.

As a bitter critic of humankind, few approach the misanthropic pessimism of Shakespeare's *Timon of Athens*. At one point, he sardonically offers gold to thieves with this curse.

Rascal thieves,
Here's gold. Go, suck the subtle blood o'th'grape,
Till the high fever seethe your blood to froth
And so'scape hanging. Trust not the physician;
His antidotes are poison, and he slays
Moe than you rob, takes wealth and lives together.
Do villainy, do, since you protest to do't,
Like workmen. I'll example you with thievery:
The sun's a thief, and with his great attraction
Robs the vast sea; the moon's an arrant thief,

And her pale fire she snatches from the sun;
The sea's a thief, whose liquid surge resolves
The moon into salt tears; the earth'a a thief
That feeds and breeds by a composture stol'n
From gen'ral excrement-each thing's a thief.
The law, your curb and whip, in their rough power
Has unchecked theft. Love not yourselves; away,
Rob one another. There's more gold. Cut throats;
All that you meet are thieves; to Athens go.

Jeremiahs hope to improve mankind by their lamentations. Timon is beyond any hope of change.

Since the world has never approached universal peace and prosperity, jeremiads are the substance of many contemporary sermons, columns, and editorials.

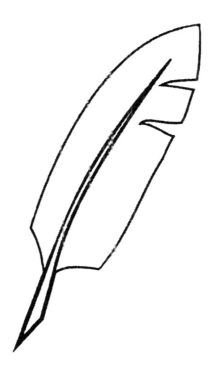

Kinesics

The subtle creases of a grimace tell the same story around the world, to preliterate new Guinea tribesmen, Japanese and American college students alike. Darwin knew it all along, but now there's hard evidence that culture does not control the face.

—Paul Ekman

The American Heritage Dictionary defines **kinesics** as "the study of nonlinguistic bodily movements, such as gestures and facial expressions, as a systematic mode of communication." No student of language should fail to explore the importance of this often misunderstood area.

Some bodily motions are indeed influenced by culture. These are intentional, not involuntary. Affectionate tongue wagging in Tibet, for example, is a friendly greeting under the control of the greeter. Such customs vary from culture to culture. Not understanding this type of communication can cause problems for tourists. Though some of these seem universal, like holding up the palm of the hand to signal "Stop," others are unique to the area. To signal agreement, Bulgarians wag their heads from left to right, not up and down.

Some body motions, especially those dominated by the muscles of the face, are involuntary, not influenced by culture. The primary emotions are linked to the muscles of the face. A study sponsored by Paul Ekman presented photographs of six faces expressing specific emotions, "happiness, fear, surprise, anger, disgust, and sadness. These were shown to college students from Japan, Brazil, Chile, Argentina, and the United States. Judgments were highly accurate and common to all five groups. Even the preliterate cultures of Borneo and New Guinea did well in matching faces with stories told them."

That corny old song perhaps said it best: "Your lips tell me no-no, but there's yes-yes in your eyes."

Involuntary reactions go beyond facial expressions. Uncontrolled motions of the entire body can signal elation, grief, astonishment, or a dozen other emotions. A shrug of the shoulders, a clenched fist, a thoughtful nod can all send powerful messages without words. These together with your facial expressions, provide clues even without words. Babies become adept early at reading kinesic signals. They quickly distinguish between a frown and a smile and respond in their own kinesic ways. Household pets read their owners' moods and are themselves affected.

Nonverbal communication is a larger category. It includes the kinesic signals discussed above. It also includes signs and symbols. Because they do not depend upon language, universal traffic signals control the flow of traffic and the behavior or motorists.

Paradoxically, one of the most effective means of nonverbal communication is silence. It can isolate us from others, induce a puzzled reaction, or mend relationships that have deteriorated. Alwin Thaler's *Shakespeare's Silence* analyzes the silences at critical moments in Shakespeare's plays. These reveal more about the characters than language. As J. Vernon Jensen has noted, "Silence can communicate scorn, hostility, coldness, defiance, sternness and hate; but it can also communicate respect, kindness, and acceptance." Potentially both balm and irritant, silence definitely affects us. Silence shatters a person in solitary confinement, but to a harried young mother, silence soothes."

Sign language, the language of the hearing-impaired, is a brilliant example of nonverbal metaphor. It combines kinesic signals with nonverbal signs and symbols. American Sign Language, *Ameslan*, cleverly uses the body and symbols to convey a message. Here's a graphic illustration of the ingenious strategy, as described by Ruth Brown: "Flick your right index finger upward next to your forehead, then form an 'O' in mid-air with your cupped hand before pointing to yourself. That would convey in *Ameslan*, 'understand zero me' or in English, 'I don't understand a single thing.'"

128

"Perhaps most of the expressions of emotional motivational states occur on nonverbal levels." A study, reported by Philip V. Lewis, notes "during the course of the day we blush, sweat, gasp, chock, cough, twitch, squirm, scratch, blink, fidget and wiggle...A suppressed smile, a lifted eyebrow, or a wrinkling of the nose can serve as a barometer of how the speaker feels about that he is saying or, alternatively, how he is reacting to what is being said."

The study of language is ancient. By comparison, the study of kinesics is recent.

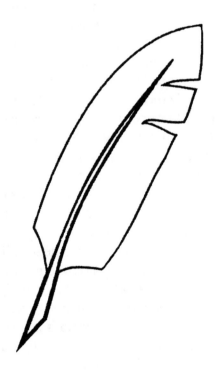

Lexicography

Lexicographer-a writer of dictionaries, a harmless drudge, that busies himself in tracing the original, and detailing the signification of words.

—Samuel Johnson

For the maker of dictionaries, Dr. Johnson's wry comment is not far from the reality. The laborious collection of citations is at the heart of every dictionary. Finding the earliest written use of a word and following the trail to contemporary usages has fascinated lexicographers to the present day.

In the history of dictionary making, Dr. Samuel Johnson is a giant, but he was by no means the first. A kind of dictionary was found in the library of the Assyrian King Ashurbanipal, who reigned in the seventh century B.C.E. in Mesopotamia. Dictionaries appeared in England before Johnson's massive two-volume tomes in 1755. Johnson's dictionary was so inclusive, so creative, so original, however, that it remained the standard for many years after his death.

Half a century later, in 1806 Noah Webster published *A Compendious Dictionary of the English Language*, a thoroughly American dictionary that demonstrated the strength and vitality of American English. He introduced or supported spellings that have persisted since his time: *honor* for *honour*; *frolic* for *frolick*; *center* for *centre*; *traveled* for *travelled*; *defense* for *defence*. He hoped to go further with the implified spelling, based on pronunciation, but words like these never took on: *nebor*, *porpess*; *sew* to *soe* and *soot* to *sut*.

The third landmark dictionary is *The Oxford English Dictionary*, first discussed in 1857 This was to be "A New English Dictionary" on a historical basis. For each word, the earliest citation would be found, noted, and dated. Subsequent citations would be used to derive the definition(s) that appear in the dictionary.

Editions were published alphabetically, as completed. The first volume, A-B, appeared in 1884. Because of its scope and size, the final copy, volume 12, appeared in 1928.

The *OED* is also published in an abridged edition, the *Shorter Oxford English Dictionary*. The word *shorter* is relative. The two-volume version contains 3,792 pages and attempts to incorporate words that have entered the language since 1993. The interval produced 3500 new words for inclusion. Angus Stevenson, the new edition's co-author, declared, "With technology and the speed of communication, new words and usages become established much more quickly" than in previous times. Some of the new words include *wannabe*, *body-piercing*, *lipectomy*, and *Prozac*. Science fiction has provided *dilithium*, *warp drive*, *dark side*, and *mind meld*. An ominous word like *Taliban* makes the new edition. The impact of technology is discussed in "*Neologisms*."

When will this 2002 edition have to be revised!

There have been other dictionaries, of course, but none with the ambitious scope of the *OED*.

A major problem of dictionary makers is to decide whether the emphasis should be principally prescriptive or descriptive. Simply put, should we present the language as it should be (at least according to our standards) or as it actually is? The latter approach, the historical, doesn't preach, but also doesn't help with advice on surviving society. One problem with the former approach, the prescriptive, is setting forth rules that are unrealistic in changing society Most dictionaries try to meet both needs, with cautiously worded comments on usage along with definitions that describe while minimizing judgments.

Limerick

There was an old party of Lyme,
Who married three wives at one time.
When asked, "Why the third?"
He replied, "One's absurd,
And bigamy, sir, is a crime.
                              —William C. Monkhouse

The **limerick** is a popular verse form often used for witty observations, daring rhyming, or raunchy commentary. It's a concise form: three four-syllable rhyming lines and two three-syllable rhyming lines. The first four lines set the stage and the fifth line provides the punchline.

Most limericks by anonymous authors find their way into popular culture. A classic, met by most people at some time, is this:

There was a young lady of Niger
Who smiled as she rode on a Tiger;
They came back from the ride
With the lady inside
And the smile on the face of the Tiger.

Some limericks carry nonsense to new heights (or depths!):

There was a young lady of Venice
Who used hard-boiled eggs to play tennis;
When they said, "You are wrong,"
She replied, "Go along,
You don't know how prolific my hen is."

There was an old man from Peru,
Who dreamed he was eating his shoe.
He woke in a fright
In the middle of the night
And found it was perfectly true.

And an example of the only slightly naughty:

There once was a sculptor named Phidias,
Whose statues by some were though hideous;
He made Aphrodite
Without any nighty,
Which shocked the ultra-fastidious.

Among creators of limericks, Carolyn Wells holds an honored place.

A Tutor who tooted the flute
Tried to teach two young tutors to toot;
Said the two to the Tutor
Is it harder to toot, or
To tutor two tooters to toot?

The origin of the limerick is obscure, with three competing sources suggested, connected in some way with the Irish city of Limerick. Although not a major literary form, the limerick has been popular for nearly three centuries. It can be (and often is) ribald, but it can also be quite innocuous like the Tiger limerick quoted above.

Lost Languages

The story of language is the story of human civilization. Nowhere is civilization so perfectly mirrored as in speech...It is the basic foundation of all human cooperation, without which no civilization is possible.

—Mario Pei

A study of language is basic to a study of culture. When Linear B., the language of ancient Crete, was finally deciphered in 1952, elements of the Minoan culture came into sharper focus.

Languages are mortal. The number of living languages is constantly decreasing. Language experts have estimated that half of the world's 6,800 languages could die by 2100. Why worry? When a language dies, a culture dies with it. The world becomes more homogeneous, less diverse.

Half of current languages are spoken in eight countries: Papua New Guinea, Indonesia, Nigeria, India, Mexico, Cameroon, Australia, and Brazil. Many of all remaining languages have few speakers, the number diminishing as the elders die off. To pass from generation to generation, languages need at least 100,000 speakers, unfortunately half of all languages are spoken by fewer than 2,500 people each. Eyak, spoken in Alaska's Prince William Sound, is down to one speaker!

Not all endangered languages are in Third World countries. In the United States, Navajo is threatened. In the British Isles, Cornish needs renewal to survive.

Languages sometimes experience a revival because of nationalistic impulses; for example Hebrew in Israel and Celtic (or Irish) in Ireland. New nations sometimes see in their linguistic past evidences of former glory and qualities worth renewing. Revival of a former language may inspire a new patriotism.

"Dead" languages like Latin may survive in ritual and in the many offshoots in related languages.

Malapropism

> *I would never let her meddle with Greek,*
> *or Hebrew or such inflammatory branches of*
> *learning.*
>   *She should have a supercilious knowledge*
> *in accounts. —As she grew up, I would have*
> *her instructed in geometry, that she might*
> *know something of the contagious*
> *countries…and likewise that she might*
> *reprehend the true meaning of what she is*
> *saying…This is what I would have a woman*
> *know; —and I don't think there is a*
> *superstitious article in it.*
>   —Richard Brinsley Sheridan

The speaker, Mrs. Malaprop, a key figure in the play *The Rivals*, is here giving her philosophy of raising and educating a young woman. The alarming unintentional misuse or distortion of a word has given the invaluable word **malaprop** to the language (*mal-apropos*: *not suitable*). Mrs. Malaprop doesn't stop here. She peppers her speeches in the play with other glorious examples.

> *Illiterate him, I say, quite from your*
> *memory.*
>   *If I reprehend anything in this world, it is*
> *the use of my oracular tongue, a nice*
> *derangement of epitaphs.*
>   *She's as headstrong as an allegory on the*
> *banks of the Nile.*
>   *No caparisons, miss, if you please.*
> *Caparisons don't become a young woman.*

Sheridan didn't invent malapropisms, but he provided a colorful and convenient label for the ludicrous misuse of language. Long before eighteenth-century drama, Shakespeare was exploiting that source of humor. The Shakespearean master of the malaprop is constable Dogberry in *Much Ado About Nothing*. At one point he declares, "Does thou not suspect my place? Dost thou not suspect my years?" When he captures the villains he exclaims, "O villain! Thou wilt be condemned into everlasting redemption for this." There are other malaprop artists in Shakespeare. Mistress Quickly in *The Merry Wives of Windsor* declares that George Page has "a marvelous infection to the little page." In *Measure for Measure*, Constable Elbow arrests two notorious "benefactors" and "detests" that his wife is honorable.

Malapropisms and tortured English are a source of humor on television, too. Among the classic abusers of language are Gracie Allen and Archie Bunker. In real life, baseball managers Yogi Berra and Casey Stengel and Hollywood magnate Sam Goldwyn are famous for their creative misuse of language. When Berra was asked if he had made up his mind about taking a job as manager of the Mets, he said, "Not that I know of." Another coach commented about a close game: "That certainly was a cliff-dweller." Goldwyn's "Include me out" has become classic. Everyday conversation sometimes produces examples: "I was so hungry I gouged myself." Or "Dogs bark. It's only human nature."

John Sherwood collected malapropism from his readers:

> *I'm as nervous as a wreck.*
> *I waited on him hand and glove.*
> *He shook like an aspirin leaf.*
> *The papers were waylaid somewhere.*
> *He's slight of hearing.*
> *That bid certainly took the steam out of my sails.*

Alexander Pope said, "A little learning is a dangerous thing." The saying may apply to malapropisms.

Maxim

All life is an experiment. Every year, if not every day, we have to wager our salvation upon some prophecy based upon imperfect knowledge.

—Oliver Wendell Holmes, Jr.

People prefer wisdom in small packages, easy doses. The maxim satisfies that need. Defined as a general truth, fundamental principle, or rule of conduct, the maxim survives because it says something that many people feel but cannot articulate.

Some of the greatest writers have provided maxims, sometimes in collections. La Rochefoucauld has a rather sardonic sense of life.

Self-love is the greatest of all flatterers.

If we had no faults of our own, we would not take so much pleasure in noticing those of others.

Everyone complains of his memory, and no on complains of his judgment.

The English poet Oscar Wilde displays a similar sensibility.

There is only one thing worse than being talked about, and that is not being talked about.

What is a cynic? A man who knows the price of everything, and the value of nothing.

The only way to get rid of a temptation is to yield to it.

Benjamin Franklin often strikes a more positive note.

> *Do not anticipate trouble, or worry about what may never happen. Keep in the sunlight.*

> *Dost thou love life? Then do not squander time; for that's the stuff life is made of.*

> *Human felicity is produced not so much by great pieces of fortune that seldom happens, as by little advantages that occur every day.*

T-shirt slogans and bumpers stickers provide some contemporary, often risqué, messages.

> *A journey of a thousand miles begins with a cash advance.*

> *Quoting one is plagiarism. Quoting many is research.*

> *My wild oats have turned to shredded wheat.*

Synonyms of *maxim*, include *proverb*, *adage*, *aphorism*, *saying*, and *epigram*. A **proverb** is an anonymous statement of a general truth, usually in simple language: "A fool and his money are soon parted." An **adage** is an old saying generally accepted as true. An **aphorism** leans toward profundity, rather than simplicity. A **saying** is general, not necessarily wise. It tends to be current, sometimes timely, often fleeting.

An **epigram** is a "tense, sage, or witty and often paradoxic saying." Memorable and frequently quoted, it often has a life of its own. A good example is Oscar Wilde's "The only way to get rid of a temptation is to yield to it."

Metaphor

Two butterflies went out at noon
And waltzed above a stream
                                                            —Emily Dickinson

Emily Dickinson has taken a stately dance and the butterfly's flight and linked them in an arresting image. A new and creative image requires a flash of insight.

Of all forms of figurative language, **metaphor** is the most common, most pervasive, most profoundly important. The dictionary defines *metaphor* as an implied comparison. It takes two more or less unrelated items and links them together: *waltz, butterfly's flight.*

Poets use metaphor in startling ways, but they don't have a monopoly on metaphors. Everyone uses them- constantly. Action metaphors are common: *find an excuse, drop a hint, grasp at an opportunity, demolish an argument, lift one's spirits, fly into a rage.* When we're depressed, we're *down.* When we're happy, we're *on cloud nine.*

Metaphors are everywhere. We use parts of the body for comparisons: *the teeth of a storm, the eye of a hurricane, the arm of the sea,* the *Finger Lakes,* the *shoulder* of a mountain, the *nose* of an airplane, a *head* of cabbage, a *leg* of the chair, the *jaws* of a clamp, an *ear* of corn, a *neck* of the woods, the *mouth* of the river.

Flower names are especially fruitful (itself a metaphor); b*irds-foot violet, goldenrod, black-eyed Susan, buttercup, cat-tail, dewdrop, milkweed, tiger lily, wake-robin, snakeroot, Queen Anne's lace, fireweed, honeysuckle, jewel weed.* Sometimes the image is pungent, rather than sweet: *skunk cabbage.*

In addition to these more obvious examples, concealed metaphors enrich our language. Often the comparison is hidden in a word's history. According to its etymology, an aster is a *star*, a dandelion is a *lion's tooth*, a pansy is a *thought*, a geranium is a *crane's bill*, an anemone is a *wind flower*, an amaranth *cannot fade*, an amethyst *wards off drunkenness*, a hepatica leaf is shaped *like a liver*.

Metaphors may be mixed, often with humorous effect. "My candidate will 'strangle the snake of corruption and nip it in the bud.'" Sometimes major writers mix metaphors and get the reader's attention. Hamlet considers taking "arms against a sea of troubles." John Milton calls the corrupted clergy "blind mouths" and then mixes the metaphor further by adding that they "scarce themselves know how to hold a sheep-hook." This strategy is not recommended for writers below the genius level!

In a column on the newspaper publisher Katharine Graham, Maureen Dowd said about Ms. Graham, "She was the little brown hen who blossomed into a swan."

At first glance, this is clearly a mixed metaphor. Hens don't *blossom*; flowers *blossom*. Yet a case can be made for insisting that blossom has diluted its horticultural association and can also mean *simply to grow, to come into one's own, to change positively*.

"Yes," say the purists, "but even *grow* is figurative. You'd better stick to something neutral like *to change positively*."

Maureen Down might retort, "My original statement is clear, concise, and to the point. Who could worry about such a minor point?"

In a sense all language is a metaphor. *Chair* is not the object; it stands for the object…and *stands* is an obvious metaphor.

140

Metathesis

O Cuckoo: shall I call thee bird
Or but a wandering voice?
—John Keats

A parodist, possibly a teacher at exam time, wrote this wry answer:

State the alternative preferred;
Give reasons for your choice.

This chuckle wouldn't have been possible if *bird* had its Old English spelling *bridd*. The transformation of *bridd* into *bird* is a strange linguistic phenomenon. Though it is not rare and includes some of our commonest words, it has a forbidding name: **metathesis**, by derivation a "going over."

There seems to be a temptation to exchange sounds within words, perhaps because the transposition sometimes makes the word easier to pronounce. The substandard pronunciation of *modren* for *modern* seems to support that supposition. The accepted word *flimsy* may also be easier to pronounce than the older *filmsy*.

Language generalizations, however, are risky. Though the newer form seems easier to pronounce in the preceding examples, other pairs show an opposite tendency. Our word *third* doesn't seem to be any easier to pronounce than its older ancestor *thridd*. We actually retain the sound order in our word *three*, but we somehow have adopted the word *third*. Other transformed words include *wasp* (for *wapse*) and *clasp* (for *clapse*).

Language evolution can be unpredictable. The current word *curd* has been derived from an older form *crud*, just as *third* has been derived from *thridd*. But there is a difference with this pair, *crud* has also stayed on as a slang word suggesting a disagreeable deposit of filth or grease.

The word *dirt* is interesting because it has denotations and connotations up and down the scale. For the gardener, *dirt* has a positive connotation, but it has negative connotations for mothers, housemaids, and victims of gossip. In its current usage, *dirt* has a wide variety of meanings, literal and metaphorical. The original word *dritt* was more limited and specific in meaning.

In *Current English*, Arthur G. Kennedy says, "This process of metathesis is one of the features of slovenly and confused speech and is especially likely to appear in the prefixes *per-* and *pre-*." He provides examples: *perscription* for *prescription* and *prespiration* for *perspiration*. This example is especially interesting because *pre-* is substituted for *per-* in the first pair and *per-* is substituted for *pre-* in the second. Kennedy adds other forms that he labels objectionable: *perty* for *pretty*, *apern* for *apron*, *childern* for *children*. (That difficulty with the *r* sound appears in the frequent intrusion of *r* in *prostate-prostrate*.) He also mentions *calvary* for *cavalry*, *revelant* for *relevant*, and *aks* for *ask*. The last form actually has historical support. In one form of Old English it was spelled *acsian*.

Despite Kennedy's negatives, transformed words often make it into the accepted language, replacing the original "correct" form. *Bird* has replaced *bridd*, and the language is no poorer for the change.

Meter

Trochee trips form long to short,
From long to long in solemn sort
Slow spondee stalks; strong foot yet ill able
Ever to come up with the dactyl trisyllable,
Iambs march from short to long.
With a leap and a bound the swift anapests
throng.

—Samuel Taylor Coleridge

The poet here is demonstrating **meter**, the pattern of stressed and unstressed syllables in verse. In English, meter depends upon stress: a-FRAID. In poetry, lines are often divided into feet, each with at least one stressed syllable. As Coleridge demonstrated with the five most important patterns above, each pattern makes a special contribution to the sense of the verse. Here are the five most common verse patterns in easily recognized form.

Name of Foot	Number of Syllables	Syllable Accented	Example
iamb	two	second	Marie
trochee	two	first	Mary
anapest	three	third	Gabrielle
dactyl	three	first	Gabriel
spondee	two	both	Tom Jones

The following brief bits of poetry demonstrates again each meter.

Iamb. Called the *walking rhythm*, the iamb permeates everyday conversation. Shakespeare chose the iamb as the basic patter of all his poetry. He created a line of five feet: iambic pentameter- also called **blank verse**. A line of iambs only would be monotonous. Shakespeare introduced many variations. The following selection is pure iambic tetrameter (four feet):

> *About the woodlands I will go*
> *To see the cherry hung with snow.*
> > —A.E. Housman

Trochee. If the iamb is a walking rhythm, the trochee suggests running.

> *Double, double, toil and trouble,*
> *Fire burn and cauldron bubble*
> > —William Shakespeare

Anapest. If the iamb suggests walking and the trochee running, the anapest suggests galloping

> *Like a child from the womb, like a ghost*
> > *from the tomb,*
> *I arise and unbuild it again.*
> > —Percy Bysshe Shelley

Dactyl. Like the three-quarter time in music, the dactyl is almost a waltzing rhythm.

> *This is the forest primeval. The murmuring*
> > *pines and the hemlocks.*
> > —Henry Wadsworth Longfellow

Spondee. The rhythm of the spondee is the beat of marching soldiers. The spondee rarely carries a line, by itself. It is used more often for variation in other lines of poetry. The following example provides the feel of a spondaic line.

> *Break, break, break*
> *On the cold gray stones, O Sea!*
> > —Alfred Lord Tennyson

The last foot of line two is a spondee. The first line suggests the heavy beat of the spondee, though each foot apparently has only one syllable.

Note that even the lines used as models above sometimes include variations. The Tennyson selection, for example, includes an anapest ("on the cold") and an iamb ("gray stones").

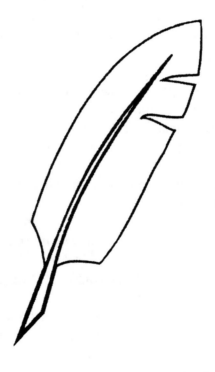

Metonymy

Beneath the rule of men entirely great,
The pen is mightier than the sword.
>—Edward Bulwer-Lytton

Metonymy substitutes one word for another closely associated. The pen is associated with the written word; the sword, with violence. Though the name metonymy may be unfamiliar, examples abound in everyday conversation: tasty *dish* (contents of dish), *sweat* equity (work done to save money, *kettle* boiling (water in the kettle).

The sports pages are gold mines for examples of metonymy. For many years Pete Sampras owned *Wimbledon* (the tennis tournament played at Wimbledon). The Lakers have a strong *bench* (secondary players). The Mets rally overtaxed the Braves *bullpen* (relief pitchers). Though the *pigskin* (football) may not be made of pigskin, the name persists.

Politics, too, spawns examples of metonymy. The *White House* (the President) and the *Capitol* (the Congress) are at odds. The British *crown* (the Queen) has provided stability through anxious times. The *backbenches* in Parliament put on a noisy display. *Russia* and *China* supported the U.N. resolutions.

Monologue-Soliloquy

That's my last Duchess painted on the wall,
Looking as if she were alive. I call
That piece a wonder now: Fra Pandolf's hands
Worked busily a day, and there she stands.
Will't please you sit and look at her?
—Robert Browning

The Duke of Ferrara, powerful nobleman of the Italian Renaissance, is speaking to an emissary from another noble family. He is showing a remarkable portrait of his dead wife. The rest of the poem reveals that he has completed an agreement to marry the daughter of the emissary's lord. But it reveals much more. The Duke's "last Duchess" (the poem's titled "My Last Duchess") is dead. The painting shows her as if alive.

What is remarkable about the poem is its self-revelation of the Duke's hauteur and cruelty. His own words reveal the tragedy. This form of poetry is called a **dramatic monologue**...There is one speaker, though we imagine the person or persons to whom the speaker is addressing the lines.

The dramatic monologue is one form of the monologue. One-man shows frequently use the monologue to tell a story, present a character, or sketch a scene. A prayer tends to be a monologue.

Monologue is a broad term. **Soliloquy** is somewhat narrower but it is also associated with a single speaker. The soliloquy represents unspoken thoughts, a person talking to himself. The most famous soliloquies are those uttered by Hamlet at crucial moments in the play. "To be or not to be" is intended only for Hamlet himself- and, of course, the audience.

The etymologies of *monologue* and *soliloquy* are the same: one speaker. *Monologue* derives from Greek roots: *mono- log*; *soliloquy* from Latin- *sol- loqu*.

In opera, the aria functions as a kind of soliloquy.

Myth

*There is a charm in the name of ancient
Greece; there is glory in every page of her
history; there is a fascination in the remains
of her literature and a sense of unapproach-
able beauty in her works of art; there is a spell
in her climate still, and a strange attraction in
her ruins...There is not in all the land a
mountain, plain, or a river, nor a fountain
grove or wood, that is not hallowed by some
legend or poetic tale.*

—Alexander S. Murray

This introduction to Murray's classic *Manuel of Mythology*,
suggests some of the appeal of myth. A **myth** is fiction, usually
dealing with a supernatural or superhuman being. Narrowly
considered, myths are concerned with stories of creation, but more
generally myths explain natural phenomenona, human qualities,
social customs, religious rites, the origins of institutions.

Greek mythology, along with its derivative and parallel Roman
mythology, accounts for most mythological references and allusions.
The literature of English speaking peoples are rich in references to
gods and heroes. A growing interest in the mythologies of other
peoples as well has enriched the study of ancient cultures.

Myths provide a storehouse of stories to draw upon. Even
the names form myths have entered the language as common nouns
from the Greek: *atlas, erotic, helium, hypnosis, odyssey, panic,
tantalize, zephyr*; from the Roman: *cereal, cupidity, Herculean,
iridescent, martial, mercurial, saturnine, volcano.*

The word *myth* has acquired other meanings, other
connotations. A fictitious story presented as true or an unscientific
account may be dismissed as a myth. The Loch Ness monster has
been rejected as a myth.

Some writers have created a mythology resembling classic

myths, with heroes, supernatural forces and other-worldly settings. J.R.R. Tolkien has created mythology, *The Lord of the Rings*, about Middle Earth and its inhabitants. Called "a gigantic myth of the struggle between good and evil," it is a completely realized world with a geography, a time scheme and delightful hobbits. These are "small, furry-footed humanoids with a delight in simple pleasures" and a dislike of "the uncomfortable responsibilities of heroism."

The *Star Trek* films and television programs have created a mythology with larger-than-life heroes and their powerful foes. George Lucas's *Star Wars* series has all the characteristics of a complete mythology.

Like myths, **legends** are narratives, often of persons whose exploits are beyond the ordinary. Legends are more likely to have a basis in fact than myth. The word *legend* is often used about recent figures. Babe Ruth has often earned the *legend* label.

An interesting use of the word is *urban legend*. Completely fictional stories arise from nowhere, explaining some mysterious situation impossible to verify. One such tells of an alligator, flushed down the toilet by a thoughtless owner, which has developed in the sewer into a man-eater.

In *Too Good to be True*, Jan Harold Brunvand lists and explains more than 200 urban legends. Though these often circulate as truth, they are usually without a basis in fact.

Names

"My name is Alice, but—."

*"It's a stupid name enough!" Humpty
Dumpty interrupted impatiently. "What does
it mean?"*

*"Must a name mean something?" Alice
asked doubtfully.*

*"Of course it must," Humpty Dumpty said
with a short laugh: "my name means the shape
I am—and a good handsome shape it is, too.
With a name like yours, you might be any
shape, almost."*

—Lewis Carroll

In *Through the Looking Glass*, Alice has a marvelous
encounter with Humpty Dumpty, who explores the insights of
General Semantics in a delightful dialogue. Here he exposes his
weakness and a common misunderstanding: that words mean
something in themselves. The print on a page and the breath of a
voice identify an individual, but they do not in themselves mean
anything, despite Humpty Dumpty.

Of course, words acquire associations that seem tied to the
letters themselves. These associations, though based irrationally,
become important. The names shouldn't make a difference, but
they do. Parents agonize over the naming of the new baby. Many
elements enter into their decision: family history, the name of a
popular movie star, a biblical personage, a desire to emphasize an
ethnic background, a beloved relative. Though their decision
shouldn't make that much a difference, it does. It may affect the
child's later life. It shouldn't, but it may!

The popularity of names is inconstant. Some names go in and
out of style quickly, leaving the field to old, tried-and-true names
like *John* and *Mary*. Others are based on current events. During
the successful years of Adolf Hitler, the name *Adolf* was given to

thousands of young German children. After 1945, the name *Adolf* dropped out of sight.

Teachers over a long career meet waves of certain names. The *Jennifers*, *Sharons*, *Nicoles*, and *Karens* may replace *Joan*, *Margaret*, and *Carol*. Boy's names, too, rocket to the top in popularity. The name *Jason* became so popular that an average class might have as many as two or three.

There is a perception that a girl's beauty is reflected in her name. The magazine *Psychology Today* put that possibility to the test. Photos of six girls, equally attractive, were posted in Tulane University's student center. The experimenter randomly assigned names to the six photos: *Christine*, *Ethel*, *Harriet*, *Gertrude*, *Jennifer*, and *Kathy*. Students were asked to rate the attractiveness of the girls pictured. *Christine*, *Jennifer*, and *Kathy* won impressively. There was a slight difference between female and male students, but both groups overwhelmingly voted for the girls they considered attractive. The voters were apparently influenced by the names. They shouldn't have been, but they were.

This study was made some time ago. Perhaps modern students might be more sophisticated. The trend in actors' names shows a lesser dependence upon how the name sounds. A half century ago Frances Gumm became Judy Garland. Nowadays actors are more likely to retain their own names, no matter how unusual: Andy Sipowicz, Arnold Schwarzenegger, Famke Janssen, John Leguizamo, Dagmara Dominozyk, Emmanuelle Chriqui, Viggo Mortensen.

Unusual names dot the news and sports pages. One article discussed three promising football players: LaDamian Tomlinson, Edgerrin James, and Deuce McAllister. In the search for individuality, traditional names may be passed over.

For other characters, writers often choose names they consider especially appropriate. Charles Dickens endowed many of his characters with names that seem to suggest their personalities: Mr. Pecksniff, Mr. Murdstone, the Cheeryble Brothers, Ebenezer Scrooge, Uriah Heep, Abel Magwich, Neville Landless. William

Shakespeare was not averse to using occasional colorful names to suggest the person's character or occupation: Doll Tearsheet, Dogberry, Justice Shallow, Justice Silence, and those wonderful country soldiers, Mouldy, Shadow, Wart, Feeble, and Bullcalf.

Once upon a time, hurricanes in the Caribbean were numbered, then someone had an idea to assign them names, in alphabetical order. Some male chauvinists, according to vocal feminists, decided that hurricanes should reflect "reality" and be given feminine names. The outcry resulted ultimately in the use of both masculine and feminine—alphabetical and alternating!

Upon learning that Romeo is a Montague, hated by her family, the Capulets, Juliet cries,

> *What's in a name? That which we call a rose*
> *By any other name would smell as sweet*

That's the way it should be, but it isn't!

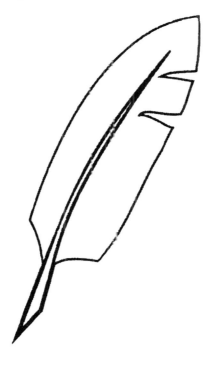

Neologisms

*Imagine downloading 128MB of music
from your PC to your MP3 player in 20
seconds. With USB 2.0, you can. USB 2.0 will
finally put the PC on equal footing with the
Mac in high-speed connectivity. USB2.0 is
rated at 480 Mbps, compared with the 400
Mbps you get with IEEE 1394 (also known as
FireWire, Sony iLINK, or HPSB), which is on
only a handful of PCs, mainly from Compaq,
Hewlett-Packard, Sony, and of course Apple
computers.*

—Bill Howard, in *PC Magazine*

All clear? If you are a computer buff, you are probably nodding with understanding. Outside that circle, there will be head shakes and confusion. Yet this quotation demonstrates how new words, called **neologisms**, get into the language. PC, for personal computer, had already established itself in the mainstream.

One of the great strengths of English is its receptivity to new words. The French are concerned with the "purity" of their glorious language, but English is not so fussy. If a new word appears and seems to make a contribution, it is soon absorbed into the vocabulary. Some words ultimately succumb to diminishing use. But some words are destined to become a permanent part of English.

The rapid spread of the computer has generated an explosion of new words and of old words used in new senses. Words like *Internet* capture the imagination of experts and "hackers" alike. Older words appear in new senses: *worm*, *Web*, *floppy*, *download*, *default*. New combinations appear: *database*, *cyberspace*, *software*, *home page*, *laptop*, *hard drive*.

New words are not confined to the computer. Popular entertainment is a source. Pop culture, through the media, introduces many new creations - a few bright and colorful.

Neologisms are not a new phenomenon. Throughout the history of the English language, new words have been added, some from foreign languages, others from native sources. Shakespeare individually created more new words than any other writer before or since. A sample of his creations: *demonstrate, emphasis, meditate, critical.*

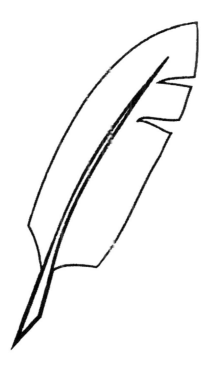

Nomenclature

Language represents the most complex behavior ever observed in any animal and certainly it's the most complex thing any of us ever learns to do. We're born into what William James calls a "blooming buzzing confusion," but by the acquisition of words we mosaic over various sectors of this blooming buzzing confusion with words.

—Terence McKenna

Language helps us to live with reality. It helps us to see differences, as between a bluebird and a bluejay. Observed differences provide useful labels that make survival possible. Having a label for poison ivy helps us avoid it. Labeling and the analysis of differences play a major role in science. Taxonomy is "the orderly classification of plants and animals according to their presumed natural relationships."

Scientists early on realized that useful, consistent labels would be needed to assure scientific progress. Attempts were made to set up categories that would put organisms into convenient boxes. To do so requires an increasing degree of specialization. The long-winged grasshopper belongs to a species, a genus, a family, an order, a class, and finally a phylum- the *arthropoda*. All have separate identifying names for the creature, but nature often resists boxes. There is occasional overlapping in the grand scheme. Some organisms "spill over." Certain one-celled organisms, for example, have characteristics of both plants and animals.

The procedure of **nomenclature**, naming newly discovered organisms, often runs into disputes and counterclaims. Having one's name incorporated into a scientific label assures a modest immortality. First discoverers have the privilege of naming, so they often incorporate their own names into the full label. For example, the dinosaur Maiakassaurus Knopfleri is named after Mark

Knopfler. Disputes sometimes arise as rivals seek to have their own labels accepted.

Obviously, a scientific name should be unique, unduplicated. But the field is vast. What happens if a new label unwittingly duplicates an older one? Syntarsus was a predatory dinosaur who lived 180 million years ago. The name *Syntarsus* had been in use for decades. Then an entomologist, Michael Ivie, found that a beetle discovered in 1869 had also been named *Syntarsus*. Here was an opportunity to override the duplicated name and rename the dinosaur. And so he did: *Megapnosaurus*. Then the dispute erupted.

True, the name *Syntarsus* had been unknowingly duplicated and could be replaced, but courtesy requires that the original namer be given first opportunity to rename the critter. That scientist, Mike Raath, had not been consulted, though Ivie insisted that he had tried to get in touch. Besides, the opponents of Ivies clamed that the new name is inaccurate. The dinosaur is only 4 ½ feet tall, scarcely *mega- big*.

Naming is increasingly difficult. In commenting on the difficulties of naming, Ivie says, "When you have millions of unknown beetles, you run out of names quite easily." This difficulty has led to a recent tendency to incorporate pop culture into the scientific names. *Bambiraptor* preyed on small herbivores, like the fictional Bambi. *Arthurdactylus connan-doylei* honored Sir Arthur Conan Doyle, author of *The Lost World*, a dinosaur fantasy. The frivolity is not reserved for dinosaurs. A type of water beetle was labeled *Tu Brutus Spangler*. Perhaps the most outlandish name was reserved for an extinct parrot: *Vini Vidivici Steadman & Zarrielio*.

Change occurs, even with common labels. Brontosaurus, giant herbivorous dinosaur of the Jurassic, captured the imagination for two generations. Children especially, loved dinosaurs, with their two favorites: Brontosaurus and Tyrannosaurus Rex. The fearsome reputation of T. Rex and the giant size of Brontosaurus made lasting impressions. Brontosaurus was almost 70 feet long, longer than two buses parked end to end. It was a popular creature in literature

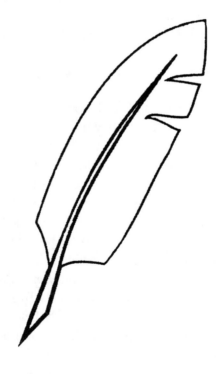

and the movies. Wilma Flintstone served Brontosaurus steaks to Fred.

In 1989, the Postal Service issued a set of four stamps featuring four dinosaurs, Brontosaurus among them. Their arrival stirred up a controversy. The purists insisted, "Brontosaurus should be Apatosaurus." They based their stand on prior labeling and confusion. The Postal Service said, "Well, yes, but Brontosaurus is still the popular name." And there the matter rests. Beloved Brontosaurus is likely to be around a long time yet. Old names die hard.

Ode

O wild West Wind, thou breath of Autumn's being,
Thou, from whose unseen presence the leaves dead
Are driven, like ghosts from an enchanter fleeing.

As thus with thee in prayer in my sore need,
Oh, lift me as a wave, a leaf, a cloud:
I fall upon the thorns of life! I bleed!

A heavy weight of hours has chained and bowed
One too like thee: tameless, and swift, and proud.
                    —Percy Bysshe Shelley

In "Ode to the West Wind," Shelley describes in vivid images the power of the West Wind. At the end, he solicits the help of the Wind to lift him from the many troubles that life has burdened him with. This is a poetic conceit. It combines some dramatic figurative language with a cry of despair. The emotional weight of the poem is contained in those final five lines.

Shelley called his poem an **ode**, capitalizing upon a long tradition. *Ode* suggests dignity and even formality. Originally, the ode was sung by a chorus as the members danced about the stage. Some poets have attempted to imitate that form, but others, like Shelley have taken liberties with the original limitations.

The serious ode often invites satire and parody. The occasional pretentiousness of the ode has often been lampooned. The 18th century poet Thomas Gray wrote a mock-heroic ode he called "Ode on the Death of a Favorite Cat (Drowned in a Tub of Goldfishes)." His language is elevated, his imagery classical, and his tone deadly serious. Like good television comics who resist laughing at their own jokes, Gray keeps up the tragic pose to the end. This is the opening stanza.

'Twas on a lofty vase's side,
Where China's gayest art had dyed
The azure flowers, that blow;
Demurest of the tabby kind,
The pensive Selina reclined,
Gazed on the lake below.

This is just a cat perched near a China vase, looking down on the fishtank. The "ode" goes on describing the cat in lofty terms, mentioning two "angel forms" (goldfish), and even remembering the traditional feline nine lives: "Eight times emerging from the flood she mewed to ev'ry wat'ry God." To no avail: the cat drowns. Gray even draws a weighty moral: "All that glisters is not gold." Poor Selina, but what a memorial! Here Gray also manages to satirize the excesses of some contemporaries.

The word ode has lost its lofty tone. A popular song may be called An Ode to…

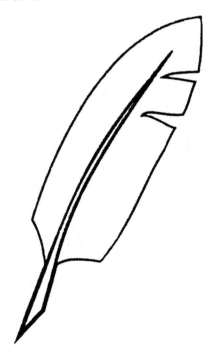

Onomatopoeia

The moan of doves in immemorial elms
And murmuring of innumerable bees.
                    —Alfred Lord Tennyson

The use of sound to suggest sense is called **onomatopoeia**. Tennyson's lines not only paint a picture; they provide the sound effects. *Murmuring* is a particularly onomatopoetic word. Other common ones include *hiss, buzz, whirring, pop, bang, whiz, clank, rattle, snap, squeak, clank, twitter, thud.*

Words like these are not uncommon. Edgar Allan Poe created a symphony of sound words in his poem "The Bells." Though somewhat overdone for many tastes, "The Bells" is a tour de force of sound effects. One stanza gives the flavor:

> *Hear the sledges with the bells- Silver bells!*
> *Silver bells!*
> *What a world of merriment their melody foretells!*
> *In the icy air of night!*
> *While the stars, that oversprinkle*
> *All the heavens, seem to twinkle*
> *With a crystalline delight;*
> *Keep time, time, time,*
> *In a sort of Runic rhyme,*
> *To the tintinnabulation that so musically wells*
> *From the bells, bells, bells-*
> *From the jingling and tinkling of the bells.*

Poe describes the sounds of other bells, each with the sound suggesting the sense.

1. *Hear the mellow wedding bells. Golden bells!*
   What a world of happiness their harmony foretells!

2. Hear the loud alarum bells—
    Brazen bells
    How they clang, and clash and roar!

3. Hear the tolling of the bells- Iron bells!
    What a world of solemn thought their melody
        compels!

This is a poem overloaded with exclamation points, but there is no denying the clever way in which the poet manipulates the natural music of English words to suggest the sense of the lines.

Onomatopoeia often depends upon a conscious imitation of natural sounds. Surprisingly, different languages interpret natural sounds differently. We may hear *cock-a-doodle-do* for the crowing of a rooster, but other languages have different words for the same sounds. The French, for example, hear *coquerico, cocorico*. Do French chickens speak differently from American fowl? The difference is in our perceptions.

Oratory

*Let every nation know, whether it wishes
us well or ill, that we shall pay any price, bear
any burden, meet any hardship, support any
friend, oppose any foe, to assure the survival
and the success of liberty.*
—John F. Kennedy

Those who listened to John F. Kennedy's stirring Inaugural Address in 1961 were proud, thrilled to be part of the grand plan suggested. But it was a hollow promise. In the years that followed, reality made the words ironic. The United States tried international activities to help the cause of peace and freedom, but the possibilities were limited. The grandiose superlatives were unattainable, scaled down, and sometimes overlooked altogether. *Pay any price* proved impossible.

Political oratory is a study in language manipulation. Promises made on the campaign trail ultimately run up against economic demands, party divisions, personality problems. Sometimes conflicting promises are made to cut taxes and increase services at the same time. Problems of the real world are often lost in the jargon of political strategy.

Political oratory sometimes generates expressions that become famous in their own right. At the Democratic National Convention in 1896 William Jennings Bryan, an advocate of free and unlimited coinage of silver, made a stirring speech that assured his nomination for the Presidency: "You shall not press down upon the brow of labor this crown of thorns. You shall not crucify mankind upon a cross of gold."

Not all political oratory is transient, inflated, high flown, tailored to expediency. In a speech at the Republican State Convention at Springfield, Illinois, in 1858, Abraham Lincoln declared, "A house divided against itself cannot stand. I believe this government cannot endure permanently half slave and half free." In its simple imagery, the "house divided" speech proved prophetic.

Oxymoron

The shackles of an old love straitened him,
His honor rooted in dishonor stood,
And faith unfaithful kept him falsely true.
                    —Alfred Lord Tennyson

In *The Idylls of the King*, the knight Lancelot has been wounded in a tournament and cared for by Elaine, "the Lily Maid of Astolat." Elaine hopes for his love, but Lancelot loves another, Guinevere, and cannot requite her devotion. The lines are notable for three examples of **oxymoron**: *honor in dishonor*, *faith unfaithful*, and *falsely true*.

By derivation, *oxymoron* means *wise-foolish* from *oxys-sharp*, *keen*, and *moros- foolish*. The word *sophomore* is itself an oxymoron, meaning by derivation a *wise fool*. The word extends beyond the schoolroom. *Sophomoric* means *immature*, *conceited*, *overconfident*.

Besides Tennyson, other authors have used oxymoron frequently and effectively. In *Hamlet*, King Claudius explains his hasty marriage after King Hamlet's death, to Gertrude: "with mirth in funeral and with dirge in marriage." John Milton describes hell in *Paradise Lost*: "No light, but rather darkness visible." The English poet Francis Thompson calls up *traitorous trueness* and *loyal deceit*.

Oxymoron is common in everyday speech: *kill with kindness*, *friendly enemies*, *bittersweet*, *thunderous silence*, *cruel kindness*, *jumbo shrimp*, *sweet sorrow*, *laborious idleness*, *lovable rogue*, *proud modesty*. A particularly interesting example is *superette- small supermarket*. A commercial ointment for sore muscles uses oxymoron for an eye-catching trade name: *Icy Hot*.

Oxymoron is often a source of humor. Drivers on Long Island, New York consider the name *Long Island Expressway* an oxymoron because the road is so often choked with traffic. During rush hour congestion, *rapid transit* seems an ironic name for the subway. During the disastrous fluctuations of the stock market, some investors considered *financial expert* an oxymoron.

An oxymoron can deliver a sharp bite in a few words and is thus a satirist's tool. Norman W. Schur defines *oxymoron* as a "figure of speech utilizing the joining of seemingly self-contradictory terms to produce the effect of irony through paradox." The previous examples suggest the self-contained contradictions at the heart of oxymoron.

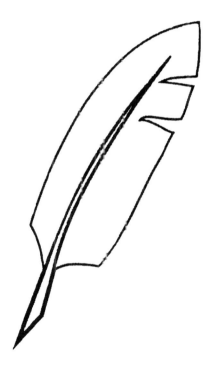

Palindromes

A man, a plan, a canal—Panama!
—Leigh Mercer

This brief tribute to George W. Goethals, chief engineer on the Panama Canal, is perhaps the most famous example of a **palindrome**. Reading the same backwards as forward, palindrome is an example of wordplay whose virtue is its ingenuity and charm.

Palindrome is derived from two Greek roots: *palin- again* and *dromein- to run*. The *palin* root also appears in *palimpsest*, a writing material used more than once- *again*. Many English words are themselves palindromes: *eye*, *gag*, *kayak*, *pep*, *pop*, *refer*, *repaper*, *wow*. All those family members join the club: *Mom*, *Dad*, *Sis*, *Bob*, *Eve*, *Lil*, *Mim*, *Nan*, and *Otto*. Among cars, *a Toyota* is a palindrome.

The challenge of palindromes requires that they make some kind of sense, even if outrageous. "Able was I ere I saw Elba" might have been spoken by Napoleon himself,—if he spoke English! A nature lover, homesick for the falls, might cry out, "Niagara, O roar again!" Tom proves to be an entomologist in "Sh, Tom sees moths." If Lew has to be told, "Lew, Otto has a hot towel," we may decide, "We'll let Dad tell Lew." Good old Otto and Hannah are favorites: "Emil asleep, Hannah peels a lime."

Some palindromes are members of a pattern.

> *"Dennis and Edna sinned." The pattern is repeated in "Enid and Edna dine." Or "Delia and Edna ailed."*

It's possible to create a clever dialogue using only palindromes. In the following, Adam is introducing himself to his new partner:
"Madam, in Eden I'm Adam."
But there is a surprise for Adam, expecting the palindrome *Eve*:

"Sir, I'm Iris!" or "Adam, I'm Ada."

Embarrassing either way.

A sample of some ingenious palindromes:
"Pull up if I pull up!"
"Ma is as selfless as I am."
"Was it a car or a cat I saw?"
"Yawn a more Roman way."
"No misses ordered roses, Simon."
"Euston saw I was not Sue."
"Noel, let's egg Estelle on."
"Some men interpret nine memos."
*"Do good's deeds live on? No, evil's deeds do
O God!"*

And this wild, outrageous one:

"I roamed under it as a tired, nude Maori."

Finally: true palindrome lovers look for palindromic dates as well as words and sentences. Every 110 years is a palindromic year: 1661, 1771, 1881, 1991. The year 1881 is special: it also read the same upside down.

Enthusiasts didn't have to wait 110 years. Only 11 years after 1991, 2002 was a palindrome. Palindromist Scott Charton suggested holding a party on 2-02-02 beginning at 20:02 and serving such delicacies as

Ham-ah!
Salad, alas!
No lemons- no melon
Yo, Bro! Free beer for boy!

Paradox

How quaint the ways of Paradox!
At common sense she gaily mocks.
— W.S. Gilbert

In *The Pirates of Penzance*, the pirate apprentice Fredrick intends to give up his piratical career on his 21st birthday. But he was born on February 29, leap year day. Though he is a mature 21, according to the calendar, he's a little boy of five.

This is a humorous paradox instantly recognizable as a quirk of language, but it gets to the heart of **paradox**; contradictions.

"I lie all the time" is a common example of paradox. If I lie all the time, then this statement must be false, but it cannot be false, for then I'd be telling the truth. The sentence sets up contradictory linguistic categories, not objects in nature. "What happens when an irresistible force meets an immovable object?" This is a problem in definition. The categories are purely verbal, existing inside our own heads.

Detective stories thrive on paradox. In Arthur Conan Doyle's "The Adventure of the Speckled Band," a young lady is murdered, paradoxically, in a locked room without any apparent access from outside.

In Edgar Allan Poe's "The Purloined Letter," the sought-after letter is concealed in the most ingenious hiding place- in plain sight. In G.K. Chesterton's "The Invisible Man," the murderer is invisible because he is so familiar that he is physically visible but psychologically invisible. The confusion is traceable to our own minds.

In life, too, many actions and experiences seem paradoxical because we fail to look beyond the verbal contradictions. A hateful recluse may be loving to his pet dog. A noted physicist may be engrossed in soap operas. A brutal football player may spend his free time playing the flute.

Paradox infects the law. Built up case by case over many

centuries, the law seeks to apply accumulated wisdom to solving specific problems, but apparent discrepancies sometimes arise. A hardened criminal may escape punishment by a technicality, while a lesser felon may receive extended jail time. Sentences depend upon personalities and legalistic interpretations, applying verbal decisions to real-life problems. Sometimes the clothes don't fit perfectly.

Modern physics avoids easy classification, defies logic, embraces paradox. "Light is simultaneously a wave and a particle." How is such a contradiction possible? Rudy Rucker has surveyed the paradoxes of physics and declared, "Reality is one, and language introduces distinctions that need not be made." Niels Bohr, Nobel Prize Winner and leading exponent of the quantum theory, said, "Great truth is a statement whose opposite is also a great truth." This principle of complementarity, as he called it, accepts the paradoxes inherent in reality. As a demonstration of this belief, Bohr introduced the Taoist Yin/Yang symbol into his coat of arms. The outer circle enfolds both light and dark and binds them together.

Parody

To have it out or not. That is the question-
Whether its better for the jaws to suffer
The pangs and torments of an aching tooth,
Or to take steel against a host of troubles,
And, by extracting them, end them?
                                    —Anonymous

Parody imitates the style of an author for comic effect or ridicule. The style of Hamlet's speech above is recognizable, but the words poke fun at the original. The parody is a literary cousin of caricature and cartoons. Exaggeration is an ingredient.

Parody didn't originate recently. The ancient Greeks were aware of it. Plato and Aristotle mention it. The playwright Aristophanes used it in *The Frogs* to poke fun at the great writers of tragedy: Aeschylus and Euripides. Many great writers wrote parodies or were themselves subjects of parodies. The *New Yorker* magazine is a current source of clever parodies.

Parody is a form of satire, bit it is limited in technique. It is perhaps more likely to be good natured than bitter. It requires some literary skill as well as an awareness of the subject's idiosyncrasies.

Burlesque is related to parody, but it tends to be more rowdy, less sophisticated. The basis of burlesque and parody is poking fun. *Travesty* was once a synonym for *parody*, but the word has come to mean an *unskilled, inept, perversion of something positive*: as a *travesty* of justice.

Patronymics

Before my body
I throw my warlike shield. Lay on Macduff,
And damn'd be him that first cries, "Hold, enough!"
—William Shakespeare

This famous challenge, uttered shortly before Macbeth's death at the hands of Macduff, is here quoted because it illustrates a common practice in surnames, **patronymics**: names derived from fathers or paternal ancestors. Patronymics are identified by some kind of tag. Both Macbeth and Macduff are patronymics with the identifying affix *mac*.

Common, easily recognized patronymics include the Irish and Scottish *Mac*, *Mc*, MacDonald- (son of Donald) and the Irish (*O'Brien*, descendant of Brien). The Russian *ich*, *vich*, *vitch* may appear as a middle name (Anton Pavlovich Chekhov). During the days of imperial Russia, the heir apparent to the throne was the Czarevitch.

The phone book reveals all the sons, perhaps the most common patronymic: *Johnson, Robinson, Thompson, Peterson, Andersen, Paulsen*, even the German form: *Mendelssohn*. A Spanish equivalent is *ez*: *Fernandez, son of Fernando*. A Welsh equivalent is *ap* or *p*: *Prichard* from *ap Richard, son of Richard*.

Osama bin Ladin and David Ben Gurion have little in common, but the patronymic *bin* and *ben* is recognizable in both. Hindi has a less familiar patronymic: *putra, Brahamputra, son of Brahma*. Genealogy buffs are crucially interested in patronymics.

Women are sometimes identified by their fathers. Nobel Prize-winning author Sigrid Undset wrote about *Kristin Lavransdatter*. *Bini* is a similar feminine form in Arabic: *Bini Ahmed*, d*aughter of Ahmed*.

Personification

The moon takes up the wondrous tale,
And nightly to the listening earth
Repeats the story of her birth.
　　　　　　　　　　—Joseph Addison

Joseph Addison fancifully comments on the moon's changing phases by personifying moon and earth. **Personification** speaks of an inanimate object or abstract idea as if it were human. Duty whispers. Truth is crushed to earth but rises again. Fear stalks the land. Love laughs at locksmiths. Justice is sometimes blind.

Personification can combine an image and an idea in an extended way:

But Faith, fanatic Faith, once wedded fast
To some dear falsehood, hugs it to the last.
　　　　　　　　　　—Thomas Moore

The cabin ran out of the forest, ran out on the shore,
And had nowhere else to run- then stopped,
Frightened, bunched up, and looked out.
Bewitched at the sea.
　　　　　　　　　　—Yuri Kazakov

Personification is a kind of figurative language, a comparison, a form of metaphor.

Point of View

Bunker Hill, 1775-1975. A granite obelisk
200 feet high commemorates the first
important battle of Great Britain against the
American rebels. Three distinguished generals,
Howe, Clinton, and Burgoyne, with 12,000
troops were besieged by an undisciplined crowd
of colonists. With great bravery the British
troops drove them from their stronghold and
occupied the heights north of Boston.
British Commemorative Card, 1975

Americans may gasp at the "inaccuracy" of the report; yet the facts are correct. What has happened? The British version stresses the valor of their soldiers and the competence of the generals. The American version stresses the victorious outcome: British failure to break the siege of Boston. In the American version, the colonists ran out of powder. The British emphasize driving off the "undisciplined colonists." By a stroke of irony, the battle took place on neighboring Breed's Hill, though the popular name *Bunker's Hill* has remained.

The importance of **point of view** is essential in assessing anyone's position, philosophy, argument, or belief. Most people are aware of this insight but forget it in the heat of argument. Because of a different readership, a newspaper's point of view influences the choice of stories, the emphases placed, and the style used. *The New York Times* and the *New York Daily News* reported on the same story with different headlines:

Drug Detective Says
Gold Failed to Prosecute Pushers

—Times

Cop Swears DA
Fixed Dope Raps

—News

The classic presentation of different viewpoints is Akira Kurosawa's film *Rashomon*. A rape-murder has been committed. We are shown the story from the different point of view of the characters involved in the tragedy. What is truth? What is reality? Which version comes closest to what really happened? Our point of view influences our understanding. Paul Newman's *The Outrage* told the story with an American setting.

In literature, point of view refers to the position of the narrator in relation to the story. The **first-person viewpoint** imagines the writer as part of the action, either as an abserver or even as a character in the story. David Copperfield begins his story with the simple "I am born."

The **third person** has several divisions. The most common is the **omniscient**. The writer feels free to present different characters, even revealing their innermost thoughts. He may jump around from place to place, relying upon his skill to provide needed unity. An author may even interject his own commentaries on the action or the characters.

The **limited third person** tells the story from the viewpoint of one character. We know only what the character knows. This is the favored method of the detective story. We go along with the chosen character, knowing only what he knows, equally surprised at the end by the detective's skill.

The rarest of all types is the **second-person viewpoint**.

> *The scar wasn't very deep. You could only see it if you were really close to her face. Like if you were going to give her a kiss on the cheek, then you could see it, but only if her hair was pulled back. If you drew a line from her earlobe to her neck, you would see where*

the scar started. It ended somewhere past her shoulder. The knife was probably dull and that was why the scar wasn't deeper. Hard to tell. She said it was nothing. And when you questioned her more she got angry. Said it had to do with love gone bad. You tried to comfort her, but she would only stiffen. Forget the sympathy, she'd say. Didn't need it. Didn't want it. Then last night, when she thought you were asleep, she left your side and quietly made her way down to the kitchen. You waited for her return. You waited. You waited. Your stomach began to churn. You got up, put on your robe and tiptoed toward the kitchen. The light was on. There wasn't a sound. You hesitated, but got up the nerve to look around the corner. There she was...as beautiful as ever. She had her hair pulled back and was putting lotion on her scar and singing gently to herself. She touched her scar like it was some kind of special orchid or fragile piece of cut glass. She looked radiant. You turned around, went back to the bedroom, packed your bags, and left.

William G. Christ

This method involves the reader in the narrative.

Authors have used mixed methods: letters, diaries, journals. In "Marjorie Daw," Thomas Bailey Aldrich tells the entire story in the form of letters. It opens with a doctor's letter and then continues in the form of correspondence between two men. This strategy combines several different first-person narratives. It even includes an omniscient paragraph to tie the threads together, gaining the sense of immediacy (first person) with the necessary information (omniscient).

Polar Thinking

It is obvious that Aristotelian logic is strictly two-valued, and, as general semanticists are fond of pointing out, so is a large part of our thinking. We tend to talk in polar terms--—the villains are all bad, the heroes all good; you are either for us or against us; you are either black or white. The allness pattern is quite apparent in the two-valued orientation. The general semanticist advocates the multivalued orientation, the introduction of degree thinking. How bad, how good, what degree of guilt, how dark, what shade of gray, how slow, how much for me, how much against me?

—Harry L. Weinberg

The multivalued orientation requires greater flexibility, greater sophistication, closer adherence to the multiple possibilities in any argument. Mutlivalued thinking avoids easy labels, unprovable generalizations, and sweeping all-or-nothing conclusions. Mutlivalued approaches to discussion are more likely to bring light to a murky problem.

Polar thinking says, "I'll either take a plane or Amtrak." Multivalued thinking points our other possibilities: the bus, driving a private car. Some persons live solely in a polar world, with simplified explanations and stubborn beliefs.

Is polar thinking bad, despite its limitations? Not at all. As S.I. Hayakawa says, there are times "when the two-valued orientation is almost unavoidable. There is a profound 'emotional' truth in the two-valued orientation that accounts for its adoption in strong feeling, especially those that call for sympathy, pity, or help in a struggle." In wartime, polar thinking is inevitable.

Polar thinking has deep roots. A nerve either fires or it does not. In the digital age, electrical impulses are either on or off. Even when we have used multi-valued thinking, we often ultimately state the problem in polar terms: "Should I buy that Subaru or not?"

Both methods of thinking are helpful in their place. Multivalued thinking operates best on a verbal level, where words are shifting, individual, easily misused and misunderstood. Most arguments would benefit from multi-valued approaches. Polar orientation seems to operate best on the biological level. When action is required, polar thinking provides the stimulus.

In a fitting sense of irony, this entry uses polar thinking in setting up the problem: two-valued orientation versus multi-valued orientation. But the thrust is not *either-or*.

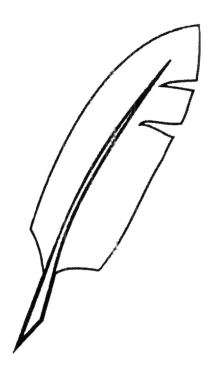

Portmanteau Words

> *'Twas brillig and the slithy toves*
> *did gyre and gimble in the wabe:*
> *all mimsy were the borogoves,*
> *and the mome raths outgrabe.*

—Lewis Carroll

This quatrain begins Lewis Carroll's classic nonsense poem "Jabberwocky," in *Through the Looking Glass*. Martin Gardner has said of it, "Few would dispute the fact that 'Jabberwocky' is the greatest of all nonsense poems in English." Carroll's inventiveness and whimsy appear in the many words he created. *Slithy* in the example quoted is especially interesting to students of language because it demonstrates a powerful tendency in language: the blending of two words to make one word with characteristics of both. Humpty-Dumpty later called words like this **portmanteau words**: "two meanings packed up into two words," in this instance *lithe* and *slimy*.

Such portmanteau words, often called **blends**, abound in English. *Smoke* and *fog* blend to become *smog*. *Breakfast* and *lunch* come together as *brunch*. *Television* combines with *marathon* for *telethon*; *motor* plus *cavalcade* for *motorcade*. Other examples: *motor* plus *hotel* = *motel*; *automobile* plus *omnibus* = *autobus*; *beef* plus *buffalo* = *beefalo*. One of the most notorious examples is *gerrymander*, a blend of *Gerry* and *salamander*. A gerrymandered district was created for politically strategic reasons while Elbridge Gerry was governor. The shape of this artificially created district resembled that of a salamander.

Blending is a historical process. Common English words were created centuries ago by blending two different words. A sample: *bat* plus *mash* = *bash*; *flame* plus *glare* = *flare*; *gleam* plus *shimmer* = *glimmer*; *smack* plus *mash* = *smash*.

Some blends are ingenious, like the combination of *anecdote* and *dotage* to create *anecdotage*, suggesting the garrulity of old age. Some blends are created by advertisers to catch the consumer's attention: *shrimply delicious*. These usually die away.

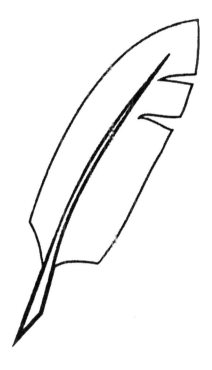

Pronunciation

*Speak the speech, I pray you, as I pronounced
It to you, trippingly on the tongue, but if you
mouth it as many of your players do, I had as
lief the town-crier spoke my lines.*

—William Shakespeare

Hamlet's advice to the players still makes sense in ordinary conversation. Correct **pronunciation** and articulation are essential for successful oral communication.

The connection between spelling and pronunciation is treated in the "Spelling" entry. Some of the difficulties caused by the lack of correspondence between the written and the spoken word are considered there. This entry deal with pronunciation.

Pronunciation has changed drastically since early Anglo-Saxon days. Until the time of Chaucer, English was fairly phonetic. The symbols represented the sounds fairly well. For example, *e* in words like *stone* was sounded. The suffixes in words like *pierced* and *frowned* were pronounced, creating words of two syllables. The lines of Chaucer's *Canterbury Tales* have a wonderful lilt because of the full pronunciation of words like these.

Between Chaucer and Shakespeare, however, pronunciation underwent drastic changes, partly because of the "Great Vowel Shift." In Chaucer, the letter *e* was pronounced like the *e* in *they*, the *i* in *kine* like the *ee* in *keen*. The Shift increased the discrepancy between sound and sense.

Vowels have changed ever since Shakespeare's day. A comparison suggests the evolution of vowel sounds over the centuries.

Today	Chaucer	Shakespeare
bite	beet	bait
about	about	aboat
beat	bet	bate
abate	abaht	abet

There were no tape recorders in Shakespeare's day. How can we infer how Shakespeare pronounced the vowels and accented his words? Scholars rely on internal evidence. If Shakespeare rhymed *serve* with *carve* and *convert* with *art*, we may reasonably assume that *serve* was pronounce "sarve" and *convert* "convart." Queen Elizabeth, Shakespeare's contemporary, actually wrote "wark" for *work*, "parson" for *person*, and "defar" for *defer*, suggesting that she wrote what she heard. Over the centuries those pronunciations disappeared, though the modern British "clark" for *clerk* and "Darby" for *Derby* are remnants.

In some ways, modern American English is closer to Shakespeare's usage than the British. *Secret'ry*, *diction'ry*, and *necess'ry* are modern British pronunciations. Americans still provide the secondary stress in these words: *dictionary*, *necessary*, *secretary*. How do we know the American usage is closer to Shakespeare's? Scanning a line from *Hamlet* clearly indicates that *customary* was pronounced in the American way, not *custom'ry*:

Nor customary suits of solemn black.

Oscar Wilde once observed, "We and the Americans have much in common, but there is always the language barrier." Differences between British and American pronunciations have long been the stuff of comedy. The stage Englishman and the stage American have provided unsophisticated laughter. Even accomplished writers on either side of the Atlantic sometimes get it wrong in trying to reproduce the speech of the other.

Oddities and inconsistencies abound in comparing American and British English. The letter *a* is a frequent source of differences. Consider the sentence "The calf came down the path to take a bath." Most Americans use the flat *a* of cat but the upper-class English employ the long *a* of father.

To American ears, the British pronunciation seems highbrow,

yet as late as 1791 an English pronouncing dictionary classified the broad *a* as vulgar. At the time, as Lincoln Barnett points out, the flat *a*, our own *a*, was considered "characteristics of the elegant and learned world." The origins of the broad *a* were Cockney. By the middle of the nineteenth century, the upper class would say "The cahf came down the pahth to take a bahth."

The consonantal sound *r* also has a fascinating history. By the end of the 18th century, it had largely disappeared in words like *bar*, *card*, *regard*, and so on, sounding very much like *baa*, *caad*, and *regaad*. This mannerism was transplanted to America by the settlers of New England. Now this fossil has been retained by Bostonians: "I paaked my caa in Haavaad yaad."

Language often disdains logic. The British pronounce chauffeur in the French way: Chauf-FEUR. The Americans prefer CHAUF-feur. Does that mean that Americans reject all French pronunciations? Not at all. The Americans prefer the French pronunciation- ga-RAGE. The British prefer GAR-age.

Portions of the United States and Canada retain pronunciations of another day. There are secluded patches of the Southern Highlands where the speech of the rural folk wouldn't sound too strange to Shakespeare.

Although the media have tended to standardize pronunciation, dialectal differences still prevail. A West Virginia woman declared, "I like to hear my mother-in-law speak. I love her New York accent." The mother-in-law made the same comment about her daughter-in-law with *West Virginia* substituted for *New York*. Though diverse, American English is not nearly so diverse as pronunciations in England, where a Yorkshire farmer has trouble understanding a London Cockney, and vice versa.

Prose

> *"For more than forty years I have been talking prose without knowing it."*
>
> —Moliere

This famous line from *The Bourgeois Gentleman* is often quoted in discussing the difference between **prose** and verse. The speaker is Monsieur Jourdain, a tradesman who aspires to become a gentleman. He hires a number of tutors to teach him how to become a gentleman. The philosophy tutor informs Jourdain that he, Jourdain, had been speaking prose all his life.

Is every sentence uttered by M. Jourdain really prose? Maybe not. In his article in the *Encyclopedia Britannica*, Edmund Gosse defined *prose* as all forms of careful literary expression which are not metrically "versified." Gosse inserts the word *careful* to distinguish "prose" from ordinary writing and speaking. The dictionary makes no such distinction, defining prose as "ordinary speech or writing, as distinguished from verse."

Most critics can, in general, agree on whether or not a selection is prose, poetry, or verse. This book is written largely in prose. By contrast "I wandered lonely as a cloud" is universally considered poetry. "Jack, be nimble; Jack, be quick; Jack, jump over the candlestick." is verse. Some classifications are easy, but there are problems along the edges.

At one point, Hamlet explains his melancholy:

> *This goodly frame the earth seems to me a sterile promontory, this most excellent canopy the air, look you, this brave o'erhanging firmament, this most majestical roof fretted with golden fire, why it appeareth nothing to me but a foul and pestilent congregation of vapours.*

This is written as prose, but few poems are more "poetical." It has no discernible meter, but there is a subtle, irregular rhythm that carries the passage along. The lines between poetry and prose are difficult to draw. Labels such as *prose poem* and *poetic prose* shed little light. Ultimately, the reader or listener must decide whether a given selection can be labeled as poetry or prose. The distinguishing features between poetry and verse are even more debatable, depending upon subjective judgment for an appraisal.

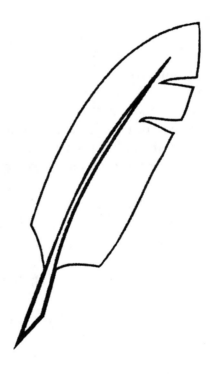

Protagonist-Antagonist

MEPHISTOPHILIS. *Faustus, this or what else*
thou shalt desire,
Shall be performed in the twinkling of
an eye.
(Re-enter Helen of Troy)
FAUSTUS. *Was this the face that launched a*
thousand ships.
And burnt the topless towers of Ilium?
Sweet Helen, make me immortal with a kiss.
—Christopher Marlowe

This scene from the Temptation of Faust is a concise illustration of the terms **protagonist** and **antagonist**. The protagonist is the leading character in the literary work. The antagonist is the one who opposes the protagonist. In the quoted example from *The Tragical History of Dr. Faustus*, the playwright Christopher Marlowe has brought the two characters face to face. Mephistophilis has persuaded Faustus to give up his immortal soul for 24 years of unrestricted pleasure. The final scene, in which Faustus is indeed carried off to hell, is powerful even in a sophisticated age. The poetry, iambic pentameter raised to greatness by Shakespeare, is brilliant. The Chorus (*see "Greek Chorus"*) has the final commentary.

Cut is the branch that might have grown full straight,
And burned is Apollo's laurel bough.

The derivation of both words is illuminating. *Pro* and *anti* are common prefix antonyms. *Agon* is the Greek root for struggle, contest. An antagonist struggles against the protagonist. A related word is *agony*.

Pun

> *They went and told the sexton and the*
> *sexton tolled the bell.*
>
> —Thomas Hood

Thomas Hood's famous example of a **pun** illustrates the characteristic play on words. This type of language fun has an ancient history. More than two millennia ago in Plautus's play *The Menaechmi*, identical twins are causing havoc among the good citizens of Epidamnum. At one point the playwright comments with a pun, cleverly translated as "The Twins are giving him twinges." Shakespeare borrowed the plot for *A Comedy of Errors* from Plautus and also the punning habit. According to Shakespearean scholar F.A. Bather, Shakespeare created (or perpetrated) 1062 puns, most in his early plays. He attributes the imbalance to youthful exuberance. One of Shakespeare's most outrageous puns is Mercutio's dying quip to Romeo: "Ask for me tomorrow and you shall find me a grave man."

Puns, sometimes labeled "the lowest form of humor," have had their apologists through the ages, giants like Samuel Johnson. The essayist Charles Lamb said, "A pun is not bound by the laws which limit nicer wit. It is a pistol let off at the ear, not a feather to tickle the intellect."

Puns are everywhere. Few people can resist the opportunity to take the plunge. Judy Garland is supposed to have said, when looking at her beloved houseplants, "With friends like these, who need anemones?" In the best puns, the items are related. Anemone is a plant, like the houseplants.

Much radio and television humor depends upon puns. In one situation, a man meets a sculptor on the street. He said, "Hi you old chiseler! Still taking things for granite?" A verse from the Biblical Book of Daniel says "According to the law of the Medes and the Persians, which altereth not." This has been mined for "One man's Mede is another man's Persian."

Tom Swifties glorify punning and raise it to another level. Named after Tom Swift, a character in popular children's books 75 years ago, Swifties require a statement then an adverb punning on Tom's comment. Here are some samples:

> *"My wife's not easy to get along with,"* Tom remarked shrewdly.
>
> *"Get to the back of the boat,"* Tom said sternly.
>
> *"Quick, Watson, the needle!"* Tom said in a serious vein.
>
> *"What I like to do on a camping trip is sleep,"* Tom said intently.

A few are more subtle:

> *"Enough of your fairy tales,"* Tom replied grimly.
>
> *"You have the charm of Venus,"* Tom murmured disarmingly.
>
> *"That dog has no pedigree,"* he muttered. (Pun in the verb.)

A popular form of humor is the contrived extended paragraph with a pun as a punch line:

"There was a man who entered a local paper's pun contest. He sent in ten different puns, in the hope that at least one of the puns would win. Unfortunately, no pun in ten did."

"A group of chess enthusiasts had checked into a hotel and were standing in the lobby discussing their recent tournament victories. After about an hour, the manager came out of his office and asked them to disperse. "Why?" they asked. He replied, "Because I can't stand chess nuts boasting by an open foyer."

It took a while, but it was worth it.

186

Punctuation

*KINGCHARLESWALKEDANDTALKEDHALFANHOUR
AFTERHISHEADWASCUTOFF*

> *King Charles walked and talked. Half an hour
> after, his head was cut off.*
> —Lancelot Hogben

The pairing above demonstrates our indebtedness to spacing and **punctuation**, an ingenious invention that we tend to take for granted. The first quotation eliminates punctuation and spacing. It is almost completely unintelligible; yet this was the form of writing in ancient times and with minor modifications and some spacing, up to the 15th century.

Providing a space between words was itself a major step. The ancient Greeks and Romans generally disregarded such spacing, but about the tenth century, words began to be separated. The difference between *wee knights* and *week nights* is a semantic chasm. Though in a written sentence, the context might clear up any confusion, the separation makes meaning more accessible.

A systematic system or punctuation had to wait five more centuries. Credit for attempting to standardize punctuation in printing is usually given to the Italian family of Aldus Manutius. The Aldine editions of the classics were models of scholarly editing and careful printing. But the system of punctuation was not adopted universally overnight. A century later, the First Folio of Shakespeare, though fairly consistently punctuated, deviated from the Aldine standards. Difficulties with Shakespearean punctuation, somewhat different from our own, have continued to stir up academic debates about Shakespeare's intentions.

The situation today is more positive. Style books help standardize punctuation, so that major periodicals can present content without confusion. Rules are fairly well standardized, though minor differences still occur. Do we insert a comma before *and* in a series? Do we put titles of full-length books in quotation marks? These differences do not affect comprehension. Some authors, like Paul de Kruif, are especially fond of dashes, often where other writers would put periods, but his content is nevertheless clear.

Much humor is derived from mispunctuation. The King Charles quotation above becomes nonsense if the period after *talked* and the comma before *his* are both removed. An old exercise was often widely used to interest schoolchildren in punctuation:

> *Every lady in this land*
> *Has ten nails upon each hand*
> *Five and twenty on hands and feet*
> *And that is true without deceit.*

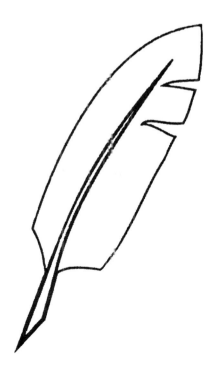

Redundancy

Madam, I swear I use no art at all.
That he is mad, 'tis true, 'tis true 'tis pity;
And pity 'tis 'tis true; a foolish figure;
But farewell it, for I will use no art.
                                    —William Shakespeare

Polonius, the garrulous old courtier in *Hamlet*, is trying to impress the King and Queen, but his message suffers from a bad case of **redundancy**: using more words than necessary. Here the disease is made worse by a repetition that adds nothing but confusion to the communication. The Latin roots provide a clue to the meaning of redundancy: *re-* back and *unda-* wave. Redundancy is a return, a repetition.

Jargon and **doublespeak** often include redundancy. Common expressions may conceal redundancy. Some critics object to expressions like *free gifts* (what else would they be?), *see with my own eyes* (how else), *a new record* (a record is new), *past history* (what else could it be?), *most unique* (but unique is one of a kind), *eyes examined while you wait* (not really an option!).

Some redundancies are so common as to raise few objections: *false pretenses*, *never before*, *joined together*, and *smile on a face*.

Related words include **pleonasm**, **tautology**, **circumlocution**, and **verbosity**. Perhaps the closest to *redundancy* is *pleonasm*. Tautology suggests repetition in different words. Circumlocution suggests an indirect, roundabout (*circa*) way of communicating. *Verbosity* is a more inclusive, less formal word. The three previous words are subsumed in *verbosity*.

Some redundancy seems to be built into ordinary communication. The columnist William Safire discusses what he calls "adverbial lapel-grabbers": *personally feel*, *manually put*, *verbally tell*, *physically put*. An expression like an *enormous giant* is a redundant emphasis.

Regionalism

> *"Well, Smiley kep the beast in a little lattice box, and he used to fetch him down-town sometimes and lay a bet. One day a feller—a stranger in the camp he was-—come acrost him with his box and says:*
>
> *"What might it be that you've got in the box?"*
>
> *And Smiley says, sorter indifferent-like, "It might be a parrot, or it might be a canary, maybe, but it ain't—it's only a frog."*
>
> —Mark Twain

In his wondrous tale of "The Jumping Frog," Mark Twain reproduces regional English, not the standard English of national newspapers or television commentators. A common meaning of **dialect** is "the form or variety of a spoken language peculiar to a region community, social group, occupational group, etc." There are other definitions of *dialect*, but this is the one considered for this entry. Some consider *dialect* a negative word, denoting inferior speech. This understanding of dialect is elitist, not supported by linguistic scholars.

A newly married West Virginia girl said of her New York mother-in-law, "I enjoy listening to her. I love her accent." The New York mother-in-law said of her new daughter-in-law, "I enjoy listening to her. I love her accent." This anecdote is true, pointing to the common feeling that the speaker's speech is standard. Elsewhere there are "dialects."

Around the country there are differences in the "music," the tone, and the phrasing of speech. Sometimes the differences are immediately apparent in pronunciation. Though geographically close to each other, New Yorkers and Bostonians pronounce words like *car*, *door*, and *water* quite differently. The speech of John Kennedy reflected the New England pattern.

Many differences in vocabulary also persist despite the homogenization of English through the media. A New Yorker in New England is amazed to hear a frying pan called *a spider*. Stanley Bank grouped some of the striking differences in vocabulary throughout the country.

> *Soda, soda pop, soft drink, tonic*
> *Living room sitting room, parlor, front room*
> *Mantel, mantel piece, mantel shelf, fire board*
> *Roller shades, curtains, blinds, window shades*
> *Clothes closet, closet, cupboard, clothes press*
> *Storeroom, lumber room, junk room, catch-all*
> *Gutter (of roof), eaves, trough, water trough*
> *Pail, bucket*
> *Frying pan, skillet, spider*
> *Faucet, spigot, tap*
> *Paper bag, bag, sack, poke*
> *Lift, elevator*

Mastering the speech of another part of the country is difficult. Native speakers develop nuances that are hard to copy. The Southern drawl, for example, is often imitated but seldom mastered outside the region. Johanna Morrison, in commenting on fake southern accents, says of true Southern speech, "It's a very hard accent to assume, actually, because it's so complicated. Even southern speech is not homogeneous." In the Outerbanks, "high tiders" speak with a cockney accent, preserved from the early settlers in that region. Similarly, the speech of the Appalachians is quite different from the speech of the coast, but also preserved from the speech of early settlers.

The speech patterns of England are even more diverse than ours. It was a major feat for Michael Caine to rise above his original cockney speech to portray an English aristocrat in *Zulu*. Fake accents can be jarring. When American actors attempt the speech of upper-class English speakers, they often fail, sometimes subtly, sometimes painfully. Similarly, an English actor portraying an American is often painful to listen to.

Regional differences add a certain charm and zest in communication, but the differences may diminish as the national media continue their pervasive influence over all speech.

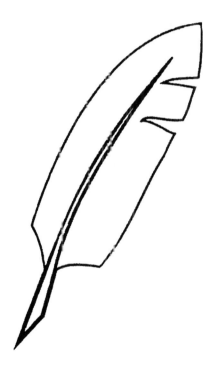

Repartee

JACK. I have lost both my parents.
LADY BRACKNELL. Both? That seems like carelessness.
—Oscar Wilde

In *The Importance of Being Earnest*, Jack has been trying to make a good impression on Lady Bracknell, the mother of his beloved and the funniest of all literary snobs. Jack regretfully announces that he has lost both his parents, Lady Bracknell, in her Olympian indifference, makes the classic response.

Repartee is a witty, clever response to another statement. Some examples have survived the years. One example involves Beau Nash and John Wesley. They met on a narrow pavement. Nash was tense and insulting: "I never make way for a fool." Wesley replied, "Don't you? I always do," and he stepped aside. A similar confrontation is ascribed to George Bernard Shaw. In this example, Shaw meets another man on a narrow staircase. He pushes his way past the other, who exclaims, "Pig!" Shaw raises his hat and replies, "Shaw. Good afternoon."

Repartee is the life blood of comedy. Entertainers like Jay Leno and David Letterman are skilled at the witty rejoinder. Sitcoms incorporate repartee in their dialogue. Comic strips feature repartee, too, often in the last panel of the strip. The popular comic cat Garfield features repartee in his relationship with hapless Jon.

Repartee is often sharp and biting, but it needn't be. Friendly repartee and banter between husband and wife can bring chuckles and strengthen a marriage.

Rhetoric

O, who can hold a fire in his hand
By thinking on the frosty Caucasus?
Or cloy the hungry edge of appetite
By bare imagination of a feast?
Or wallow naked in December snow
By thinking on a fantastic summer's heat?
—William Shakespeare

King Richard, in Shakespeare's *Richard II*, has just unreasonably banished Henry Bolingbroke. Here the banished Duke of Hereford, in anguish, expresses his dismay in a series of questions. These are not typical questions. Bolingbroke doesn't expect anyone to answer. In fact, he answers his questions himself:

O no, the apprehension of the good
Gives but the greater feeling to the worse.

A rhetorical question doesn't expect a conventional answer. It is uttered for the effect only. Sometimes it is unanswerable: "Who has solved the ultimate mystery of life?" On the other hand, sometimes the answer is self-evident: "Did we cower before Hitler's threats?"

Traditionally **rhetoric** has been a cornerstone of language instruction, one of the seven liberal arts. In the Middle Ages, the seven liberal arts were divided into the quadrivium and the trivium. The quadrivium included artithmetic, geometry, astronomy, and music. The trivium was composed of rhetoric, grammar, and logic. Rhetoric concerned itself principally with style, the art of using words effectively.

Traditionally the curriculum of rhetoric included invention, arrangement, style, memory, and delivery. Rhetoric can be abused. At one point in ancient Greece, the Sophists in their teaching overemphasized the strategy of presentation rather than soundness and truth. These were subordinated to skill and cleverness. Socrates died partly because of his open opposition to the Sophists and their corruption of the youth. Some of that negative connotation and rhetoric is apparent in one current use of the word *rhetoric*: "artificial eloquence and showiness of presentation." "Don't believe Judd's proposals. It's all rhetoric."

Isocrates, a pupil of Socrates, described the corruption of rhetoric, "the art of making great matters small, and small things great." This is a cautionary phrase for contemporary orators.

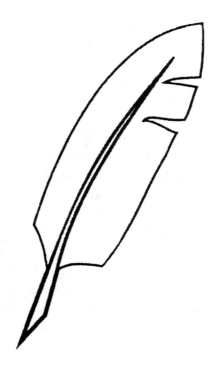

Rhyme

And while the great and wise decay,
And all their trophies pass away,
Some sudden thought, some careless rhyme,
Still floats above the wrecks of time.
                              —William Edward Hartpole Lecky

The poet pays tribute to the power of poetry, using the word **rhyme** for poetry. He also introduces rhyme into the verse. To some his quatrain (four line verse) is too glib, too facile, too unvaried in meter, but it perfectly demonstrates the role of rhyme in much of poetry.

Rhyme is a correspondence in sounds of words or syllables, usually at the ends of poetic lines.

Jack, be nimble; Jack be quick;
Jack, jump over the candle holder.

Substituting *candle holder* for *candlestick* is a jolt. The familiar rhyming word *stick* intensifies the meaning and binds the lines together.

Rhyme is an ancient element in the enjoyment of language. Nursery rhymes glorify rhyming, suggesting that children especially relate to the expected repetition of sounds.

Folklore also uses rhymes for special effects. In "Snow-White," the evil queen stands in front of her mirror and says:

Looking glass, Looking glass, on the wall,
Who in this land is the fairest of all?

In one version of the folktale "Rumpelstiltskin," the evil protagonist has made an agreement to help the miller's daughter marry the King if she will give him her first child. After the birth of her child, the new Queen regrets her hasty bargain. Rumpelstiltskin, secure in his unusual name, agrees to cancel the bargain if the Queen can discover his name in three days. Time passes. At the last minute, Rumpelstiltskin gloats at his coming victory and cannot resist dancing aloud with this rhymed incantation:

> *Today I bake, tomorrow brew,*
> *The next I'll have the young Queen's child.*
> *How glad am I that no one knew*
> *That Rumpelstiltskin I am styled.*

A servant overhears the victory chant and reports the name to the Queen. The bargain is canceled and Rumpelstiltskin kills himself in frustration.

Much humorous verse, like that of Ogden Nash, leans heavily upon rhyme. Then the identity or similarity of sounds especially delights us.

Words may rhyme within a line, not merely at the ends:

> *Then a sentimental passion of a vegetable fashion*
> *Must excite your languid spleen,*
> *An attachment a la Plato, for a bashful young potato;*
> *Or a not too French French Bean.*

In the operetta *Patience*, W.S. Gilbert pokes fun at the excesses of the esthetic movement, flourishing in England between 1870 and the mid-80s. Gilbert abhorred pretense, fads, and the petty battles of the esthetic icons. He used internal rhymes for special effects: *passion-fashion*; *Plato-potato*.

Some critics prefer the spelling *rime*.

Rhythm

True ease in writing comes from art, not chance,
As those move easiest who have learned to dance.
'Tis not enough no harshness gives offense,
The sound must seem an echo to the sense.
Soft is the strain when zephyr gently blows,
And the smooth stream in smoother numbers flows;
But when loud surges lash the sounding shore,
The hoarse, rough verse should like the torrent roar:
When Ajax strives some rock's vast weight to throw,
The line too labors, and the words move slow;
Not so when swift Camilla scours the plain,
Flies o'er the unbending corn, and skims along the main.
                                        —Alexander Pope

Alexander Pope's couplets provide a short course in **rhythm**. The lines themselves demonstrate the message being conveyed. Lines 9 and 10, for example, plod heavily along, suggesting by their heavy emphases the tortuous efforts of Ajax to throw that rock. Lines 11 and 12, on the other hand, glide swiftly along, suggesting the flight of fleet-footed Camilla, a character in Vergil's *Aeneid*.

Rhythm, the sense of movement communicated by the rise and fall in emphasis, permeates all speech. In prose or free verse, the rhythm is loose, unstructured, more or less irregular. In poetry, the rhythm tends to be more regular, often marked by metrical feet, discussed in **meter** elsewhere.

The marriage of sound, sense, and rhythm is perfectly demonstrated in Lord Byron's rollicking "The Destruction of Sennacherib." The entire poem is a powerful evocation of a bloody event told in headlong rhythm, barely allowing a reader to catch his breath. The opening stanza sets the tone and pace.

The Assyrian came down like the wolf on the fold,
And his cohorts were gleaming in purple and gold,
And the sheen of their spears was like stars on the sea,
When the blue wave rolls nightly on deep Galilee.

Human beings are ruled by rhythm—the internal rhythm of heartbeat, the external rhythms of the natural world. Rhythm, of course, plays a major role in music, with the percussion instruments helping to guide the other instruments. Throughout the world, dance has demonstrated the all-pervasive presence of rhythm.

The most sustained marriage of sound, sense, and rhythm may be Robert Southey's ambitious poem, "How the Waters Come Down at Lodore." The onomatopoetic words suggest the various sounds of the cataract, but the poem goes further, suggesting by the variation in stanza length and width, the uneven, headlong flow of the water

And thence at departing,
Awakening and startling,
It runs through the reeds,
And away it proceeds
Through meadow and glade,
In sun and in shade,
And through the wood-shelter,
Among crags in its flurry,
Helter-skelter,
Hurry-skurry.

This sample barely suggests the complexity of this tour de force. It may be overwhelming, but it is not quickly forgotten.

Riddle

I am all alone, with the iron wounded,
With the sword slashed into, sick of work and battle,
Of the edges weary. Oft I see the slaughter,
Oft the fiercest sighting

—Cynewulf

These opening lines of an eighth-century Anglo-Saxon riddle challenge the reader or listener to guess the answer to the riddle: *Shield*. It is the shield that suffers the perils listed as well as many in the lines that follow.

The **riddle** is an ancient and universal form of literature. A fascination with words has characterized speakers of all languages. There are collections of Sanskrit, Hebrew, Arabic, Persian, Latin, and Greek riddles. In size and content, riddles vary but the essence is a puzzle.

An ancient tablet, believed to date from Babylonian times, presents this riddle:

Who becomes pregnant without conceiving?
Who becomes fat without eating?
The answer is *Cloud*.

Riddles appear in fairy tales, legend, and folklore. Probably the most famous is the riddle the Sphinx presented to Oedipus: "What moves on four feet in the morning, on two feet at noon, and on three in the evening?" Oedipus solved the riddle by replying, "Man." Children crawl on four feet, adults move on two, and the aged need a cane, adding an extra foot.

The *Greek Anthology* is a remarkable collection of short epigrammatic poems from the 7th century B.C.E. to the tenth century C.E. Book 14 contains a collection of riddles, of which the following is a sample:

I am the black child of a white father; a wingless bird flying even to the clouds of heaven. I give birth to tears of mourning in pupils that meet me and at once on my birth I am dissolved into air.

The answer is *Smoke*. The pupils are those of the eye.

Some riddles have never been solved, though students have been trying for centuries.

Here's an old favorite that still challenges listeners on first reading, but yields to analysis.

Brothers and sisters have I none. This man's father is my father's son. Who am I?

Shakespeare introduced a riddle into Hamlet:

FIRST GRAVEDIGGER. *What is he that builds stronger than either the mason, the shipwright, or the carpenter?*
SECOND GRAVEDIGGER. *The gallows-maker, for the frame outlives a thousand tenants.*

Riddles have always been popular with children, who are unsophisticated enough to enjoy even a corny riddle. The following appeared in 1820 in a book for children:

The beginning of eternity,
The end of time and space,
The beginning of every end,
And the end of every place.

The answer is the letter *E*.

Riddles have interested major writers and even sparked lively curiosity. Lewis Carroll's Mad Hatter in *Alice's Adventures in Wonderland* asks, "Why is a raven like a writing desk?" Years later, Carroll provided the answer: "Because it can produce a few notes, tho' they are very flat and it is never put in with the wrong end in front." Some riddlers were not satisfied with Carroll's answer and provided other solutions. Sam Loyd, a puzzle genius, provided a better: "Because Poe wrote on both." He suggested another: "Bills and tales are among their characteristics."

Some riddles depend upon gender confusion:

> *The village minister and his wife, the school teacher and his daughter, were walking in the woods. They found a bird's nest that contained four eggs. Each of them took out an egg and yet left one in the nest.*

The usual answer: There was only one woman: the minister had married the teacher's daughter. An alternative solution demonstrates the value of punctuation. If there were a comma after teacher, there would then be two women, the minister's wife being the school teacher.

Some riddles, also called conundrums, depend upon puns for their solutions.

> *Why are the Middle Ages called the Dark Ages?*
> *Because these were so many knights.*

> *What was President Truman's explanation for his home state's popularity?*
> *Missouri loves company*

> *Where is Minute Street?*
> *Between Sixty-first and Sixty-third. (Sixty-second)*

Sometimes the riddle involves trickery.

> *If my peacock lays an egg in your yard*
> *Who owns the egg?*
> *Peacocks don't lay eggs. Peahens do.*

Some other words related to riddle are **enigma**, **puzzle**, and **mystery**. *Enigma* suggests a level of difficulty and obscurity beyond that of the riddle. *Mystery* is a broad term encompassing literary and religious connotations. *Puzzle* generates a mild curiosity and is used in ordinary speech, without necessarily expecting a solution: "I was puzzled by his actions."

In 1939, Winston Churchill, expressing his uncertainty about the role Russia would play in the years ahead, declared, "I cannot forecast to you the action of Russia. It is a riddle wrapped in a mystery inside an enigma."

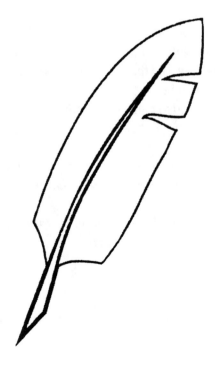

Roman à Clef

Am I alone,
And unobserved? I am.
Then let me own
I'm an aesthetic sham!

This air severe
Is but a mere
Veneer!
This cynic smile
Is but a wile
Of guile!
This costume chaste
Is but good taste misplaced!

—W.S. Gilbert

The master satirist, W.S. Gilbert, is here poking fun at the aesthetic movement, which emphasized a return to sentimental archaism as the ideal of beauty. It was often called to extravagant lengths and was accompanied by eccentricity of speech, manner, and dress. The cult was founded by the poet/novelist Oscar Wilde. The macho Gilbert couldn't stand the affectation and ridiculed it in the Gilbert and Sullivan operetta *Patience*. The central figure, Reginald Bunthorne, here confessing his deceit, is an identifiable caricature of Wilde.

When a recognizable person appears under a fictitious name, in a novel, the identifying phrase is a **roman à clef**, a novel with a key. The more general term is *livre à clef,* a book with a key).

The type can be traced to 17th century France and has been used occasionally ever since. In 1818, in *Nightmare Abbey*, Thomas Love Peacock caricatured Coleridge, Byron, and Shelley. More recently, Somerset Maugham, in *The Moon and Sixpence*, created the character of Charles Strickland, obviously a fictionalized version of the artist Paul Gauguin.

Sometimes when scandalous novels are produced for mass consumption, celebrities try to discover if they have been included under fictional names. The identification is not always a happy one.

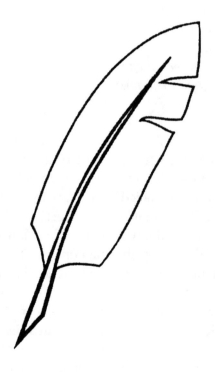

Sarcasm

GLENDOWER. *I can call spirits from the vasty deep.*
HOTSPUR. *Why, so can I. or so can any man,*
But will they come when you do call for them?
—William Shakespeare

In *Henry IV, Part One*, the Welsh rebel Owen Glendower has been boasting to Henry Percy, Hotspur, about the incredible marvels at his birth: "The heavens were all on fire, the earth did tremble." Hotspur is disgusted with the braggart's rhetoric. When Glendower utters the ultimate boast about calling up spirits, Hotspur utters the perfect retort, sarcasm at its most effective.

Sarcasm is related to satire and irony, but it is different in its primary intent to cause pain. Satire is more literary, an extended poking fun, attempting to enlighten readers. Irony is neutral. Cruelty is not central to it. Sarcasm, however, goes for the jugular. It may be suggested in the words themselves or by the tone of voice. "You're a real friend" can be complimentary or bitter, depending upon the tone of voice used.

The derivation of sarcasm provides a vivid image. The two roots are *flesh* and *tear*. Sarcasm tears the flesh. The word sarcophagus provides a related metaphor. The *sarc* root, flesh, is joined to the root *phagein*, to eat. A sarcophagus is a flesh-eater. Grisly!

Satire

The hungry judges soon the sentence sign,
And wretches hang, that jurymen may dine.
—Alexander Pope

Alexander Pope, along with Jonathan Swift, was the keenest satirist in the eighteenth century. In *The Rape of the Lock*, Pope pokes fun at the society of his day, at the vanity and affectations, the snobbery and superficiality. *The Rape of the Lock* is a mock-heroic poem in imitation of Homer or Vergil, raising the triviality of a stolen lock of hair to the grandeur of an epic like the *Iliad*. The heroine Belinda's wrath after the theft of a lock of hair provides a mock comparison with the wrath of Achilles at the death of his friend Patroclus. This is satire raised to fine art.

The heart of **satire** is protest against the follies and vices of society, holding them up to ridicule and scorn. In the couplet above, Pope is making a bitter comment about a society in which the lower classes are treated unfairly. He doesn't say so in so many words, but he contrasts *hungry* and *dine* with *wretches* and *hang*.

Perhaps the bitterest satire of all is Jonathan Swift's "A Modest Proposal," purporting to be a solution to Irish famine. He presents statistics in utter seriousness, showing the excess of children in Ireland unable to be cared for properly. Then he proposes, "A young healthy child well nursed is at a year old a most delicious, nourishing, and wholesome food, whether stewed, roasted, baked, or boiled, and I make no doubt that it will equally serve in a fricassee or a ragout." He proceeds as though he is talking about cattle, with all the economic considerations.

In grave and thoughtful prose, he explores all aspects of the possibility, point by point, declaring at the end his motive: "The public good of my country, by advancing our trade, providing for infants, relieving the poor, and giving some pleasure to the rich."

This is satire at its most powerful, shocking readers out of ignorance and complacency, calling attention to the miserable treatment of Ireland's people.

Satire is a common element in television. Programs like *Saturday Night Live* mock the foibles of politicians, celebrities, news figures, and just about everyone.

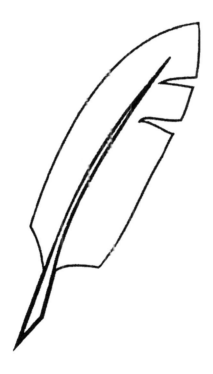

208

Self-fulfilling Prophecy

One prophesies an event, and the expectation of the event then changes the behavior of the prophet in such a way as to make the prophesied event more likely.
—Robert Rosenthal

Do we get what we expect? Very often. When the elements are controlled by us, our expectations help to bring about the desired result. Expectations of success in a given task often lead to success. Conversely, expectations of failure are likely to contaminate the effort and produce failure. Sometimes the **self-fulfilling prophesies** are generated outside the self; by parents, teachers, friends, critics of all persuasions.

Understanding this basic truth of human nature is especially crucial for parents and teachers, whose influences during the formative years is decisive. Parents who use negative labels in addressing their children or talking about them invite failure and antisocial behavior. Teachers who expect their students to be "dumb," "unteachable" consign their students in advance to failure. Unreasonable expectations can, of course, have disappointing, negative effects, but a positive approach, emphasizing realistic goals and expecting student effort, can galvanize a class. Teachers must realize that the encouragement cannot be faked. Subtle facial expressions, body language, thoughtless methodology, all contribute to the result.

The Kevin Costner movie *Field of Dreams* is an exercise in self-fulfilling prophecy. Though a fantasy, it contains a truth often confirmed in experience. "If you build it, he will come." *It* refers to a baseball diamond on a cornfield. *He* refers to a baseball player of many years ago. In this fantasy, the expectation generates the result, the return of a disgraced team, the Chicago White Sox.

An interesting illustration of the participant's role in self-fulfilling prophecy is the story of Clever Hans, the miracle horse of the early 1900s. Hans could solve different mathematic calculations and provide the answers by tapping his foot. Observers were mystified by Han's capabilities, which were indeed impressive, but not in the way the observers assumed.

There was no trickery, no intent to deceive, no observable communication between the questioner and Hans. There seemed to be no clue to tell Hans when to start and when to stop tapping his feet. The questioners were not in on any secret plan to exploit the unique talents of Clever Hans.

Ah, but there were clues that the questioners unwittingly provided, clues that they were completely unaware of. There was one basic requirement for the demonstrations. Hans had to see the questioners. Unbeknownst to all the participants, self-fulfilling prophecy was at work.

The questioners expected Hans to give the right answer, and unwittingly gave Hans the clues to perform successfully. As Robert Rosenthal explains, "A tiny forward movement of the experimenter's head was the signal of Hans to start tapping. A slight upward movement of the head, or even a raised eyebrow, was the signal for the horse to stop tapping. The horse had good eyesight, and he was a smart horse."

In the Greek myth of Pygmalion and Galatea, the sculptor Pygmalion sculpted his ideal woman and fell in love with her. When Venus turned Galatea into a living person, self-fulfilling prophecy had its ideal narrative. In George Bernard Shaw's play *Pygmalion*, the phonetic expert Henry Higgins turns Eliza Doolittle, a scruffy flower girl, into a person able to fool the aristocrats that Henry put her with. As Higgins declared, the difference between a flower girl and a duchess is the way she is treated. We tend to see what we expect to see.

Self-fulfilling prophecy was at work again.

Semantics

"Then you should say what you mean,"
the March Hare went on.
"I do," Alice hastily replied, "at least- at
least I mean what I say- that's the same thing
you know."
"Not the same thing a bit" said the Hare.
"Why you might as well say that 'I see what I
eat' is the same as 'I eat what I see.'"
—Lewis Carroll

In any discussion of semantics, *Alice in Wonderland* can provide relevant quotations, for Lewis Carroll understood the relationship between words and reality, the attempt of speakers to confine the vast world "out there" in linguistic boxes words and reality. As S.I. Hayakawa pointed out, "The semantic environment is the world of words and images in which all human beings live. It is the environment of news and information, beliefs, attitudes, laws, cultural imperatives, that constitute your verbal world and mine. A quick way of describing the semantic environment is to say that it is the part of the total environment which your pet lying on the rug has no inkling of."

The dictionary defines **semantics** as "the study or science of meaning in language forms." This study explores many areas. In *Meta-Talk*, Gerard L. Nierenberg and Henry Calero seek to go below obvious literal meanings to reveal hidden scenarios. They suggest at least three levels of meanings: "(1) what the speaker is saying; (2) what the speaker thinks he is saying; and (3) what the listener thinks the speaker is saying." When a parent replies to a child's request, "we'll see," the simple answer is a nest of meanings. (1) This is a simple reply, suggesting a later reconsideration of the original request. (2) The speaker is using the answer as an easy way to close the discussion. (3) The child understands this was a put-off unlikely to be brought up again. The simple sentence exists on many levels.

A television program examining the problems of teenagers was titled *Whatever*. This is the conversation stopper that young people use when they refuse to explore a problem, respond to a query, or have a friendly talk. *Whatever* says, "Don't bother me any further. I don't want to talk about it. I'm not sure my own thoughts are clear."

The many levels of communication were systematically studied by Alfred Korzybski in *Science and Sanity*. He coined the expression "General Semantics" and carried the subject to new levels of sophistication and comprehension. He emphasized the common confusion of words and reality. "The map is not the territory." Our mental maps do not necessarily conform to reality.

Korzybski called for more precision in communication. "I'll get there as fast as I can" would have different meanings in 1600, 1800, and 2000. Many of Korzybski's insights are explored throughout this Lexicon, in entries like "Abstract Words," "Ambiguity," "Classification," and "Formal Truths."

Simile

O, my Luve is like a red, red rose
That's newly sprung in June.

—Robert Burns

In a way, a metaphor is a compressed **simile**: A signal word, *like* or *as*, is omitted. "My luve is a rose." A simile allows a more relaxed, extended comparison. In "The Destruction of Sennacherib," Byron, writes, "The Assyrians came down like a wolf on the fold." This vivid sentence calls for a simile, not a metaphor. Samuel Taylor Coleridge suggested an ocean calm: "as idle as a painted ship upon a painted ocean."

Though not as common in speech as metaphor, simile can be used for striking comparisons. The two items being compared must, however, be different. "Tess is just like Ellen" is not a simile. "Tess is like a volcano ready to erupt" is a simile, comparing two unlike elements: Tess and a volcano.

Similes can provide vivid images in a brief space:

I wandered lonely as a cloud.

William Wordsworth

He had a voice like a coyote with bronchitis.

O. Henry

The water lay gray and wrinkled like an elephant's skin.

Nancy Hale

An irritable man is like a hedgehog rolled up the wrong way, torturing himself with his own prickles.

Thomas Hood

Many similes are old, decrepit, overused, and best forgotten: *sweet as sugar, fresh as a daisy, neat as a pin, dry as dust.*

Sonnet

SCORN NOT THE SONNET

Scorn not the Sonnet; Critic, you have frowned,
Mindless of its just honours; with this key
Shakespeare unlocked his heart; the melody
Of this small lute gave ease to Petrarch's wound;
A thousand times this pipe did Tasso sound;
With it Camöens soothed an exile's grief;
The Sonnet glittered a gay myrtle leaf
Amid the cypress with which Dante crowned
His visionary brow: a glow-worm lamp,
It cheered mild Spenser, called from Faeryland
To struggle through dark ways; and when a damp
Fell round the path of Milton, in his hand
The Thing became a trumpet; whence he blew
Soul-animating strains- alas, too few!

—William Wordsworth

In this stanza, Wordsworth provides a brief history of the **sonnet**, paying tribute to its greatest masters. The fourteen-line stanzas have been vehicles for some of the finest poetry ever created.

Why fourteen lines? The length seems particularly suited for concentrating on the message and avoiding wordiness. In another sonnet, Wordsworth paid tribute to the conciseness of the sonnet in this extended metaphor: "Nuns fret not at their convent's narrow room."

The sonnet was developed in Italy, probably in the 13th century. Its most famous practitioner was Petrarch, who brought the sonnet form to perfection. His type of sonnet is called the **Italian** or **Petrarchan Sonnet**.

The sonnet form was probably introduced into England by Sir Thomas Wyatt, a translator of Petrarch's sonnets and the creator of 30 originals. English poets found the Italian form too rigid and began creating a different form. This revised type was used by Shakespeare in his sonnet sequence. As a result, there came to be two completely different types of sonnet: The Petrarchan and the Shakespearean.

The sonnet quoted above is Petrarchan. It is divided into two parts, called the **octet** and the **sestet**. The eight-line section has two rhymes: in shorthand abba abba. The six lines are variously rhymed. Here the rhyme is cdcdee. Though the rhyme scheme is constant in the octet, poets like to play with the sestet. The two major divisions control the thought of the poem. The octet states the idea, problem, reflection, or query. The sestet provides a commentary.

The Shakespearean sonnet is quite different. It has three quatrains (four-line stanzas), each with its own alternative rhyme: abab cdcd efef. The couplet at the end is a heroic couplet (treated elsewhere), providing a neat rhyming tag to end the sonnet: gg. The three quatrains develop the idea; and the couplet at the end sums everything up.

A representative Shakespearean sonnet demonstrates the differeneces.

> *Shall I compare thee to a summer's day?*
> *Thou art more lovely and more temperate:*
> *Rough winds do shake the darling buds of May,*
> *And summer's lease hath all too short a date:*
> *Sometime too hot the eye of heaven shines,*
> *And often is his gold complexion dimmed,*
> *And every fair from fair sometime declines,*
> *By chance, or nature's changing course untrimmed:*
> *But thy eternal summer shall not fade,*
> *Nor lose possession of that fair thou ow'st,*
> *Nor shall death brag thou wand'rest in his shade,*
> *When in eternal lines to time thou grow'st,*
> *So long as men can breathe or eyes can see,*
> *So long lives this, and this gives life to thee.*

The sonnet is usually in iambic pentameter (*see "Meter"*), but poets have experimented with other meters and other rhyme schemes. Still, the division generally holds, providing examples of a form that avoids wordiness and emphasizes compression of thought.

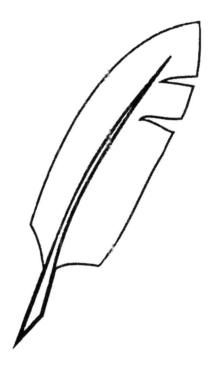

Spelling

They spell it Vinci and pronounce it Vinchy.
Foreigners always spell better than they
pronounce.

—Mark Twain

In *The Innocents Abroad*, Mark Twain, a cultured and intelligent man, plays the vagaries of spelling and pronunciation for humor. He is too critical of French spelling, and by implication, too kindly toward our own spelling. A speaker who learns the rules of French spelling and pronunciation soon finds the problem easily solved. But a foreign speaker who encounters English spelling and pronunciation for the first time is in for trouble.

Part of the problem is that 23 symbols have to represent 44 sounds. (*C*, *q*, and *x* might be omitted since other letters could cover the sounds usually represented by these.) Consider all the sounds covered by the letter *a* and other vowels.

Despite the shortage of symbols, English does quite well by assigning different letter combinations to the same sound. In the following list, a variety of letters combine to create the *sh* sound: *shoe, sugar, issue, mansion, mission, nation, suspicion, ocean, nausea, conscious, chaperon, schist, fuchsia, pshaw*.

Conversely, certain similar letter combinations, like *ough*, create different sounds: *rough, though, cough, hiccough, through, bough*. There is no phonetic help available here. The letters that make up the *ough* sound combine to create sounds quite different from the sum of the parts.

There have been humorous demonstrations of the challenges of English spelling. George Bernard Shaw suggested *ghoti* as another spelling of *fish*; the *gh* in *enough*; the *o* in *women*; and the *ti* in *fiction*. An even wilder brainstorm spells *potato ghoughpteighbteau*: *p* in *hiccough*; *o* in *though*; *t* as in *ptomaine*; *a* in *neigh*; *t* in *debt*; *o* as in *bureau*.

How did this frequent lack of connection between sound and

spelling come about? In the tenth century there was good correspondence between sound and pronunciation. Then began a period of borrowing from other languages, a process still going on. The problem was also complicated because there were a number of distinct dialects in England, each with different spellings for the same word. Although the dialect of London gradually became dominant, local dialects still had an impact. William Caxton, the first English printer, helped stabilize spelling somewhat, but he didn't supervise the spelling of the compositors he used, many of them foreign.

Attempts to simplify spelling have met with indifferent success. Perhaps the most successful reformer was Noah Webster, 18th century lexicographer. In his dictionary, he dropped the *k* from *musick*, changed *traveller* to *traveler*, *favour* to *favor*, *waggon* to *wagon*, *jeweller* to *jeweler*, *gaol* to *jail*, and *plough* to *plow*. But he wasn't uniformly successful. He tried to change *crowd* to *croud*, *acre* to *acer*, *tongue* to *tung*, and *women* to *wimmen*. Why did some of his introductions survive and not others? No one knows.

For years the *New York Daily News* made a brave attempt to replace *night* with *nite*. This is a simple change. Why didn't it take on? There is always resistance to change. Just remember the failed attempts to introduce the metric system in America. Yet some spelling changes do survive.

Although words with Anglo-Saxon roots often vary in spelling and are not phonetic, words borrowed from the Greek, though long, are usually easy to spell once the pronunciation has been mastered. Simple words like *photograph* and longer words like *tyrannosaurus* have predictable spellings. Yet even in this safe haven for spellers there are inconsistencies. We use *ph* for *phantom* and *f* for *fantastic*. Why?

Are there reliable rules for spelling? The rule for doubling consonants in *referred* but not *reference* works most of the time. The old favorite about putting "*i* before *e* except after *c* or when sounded like 'ay' as in *neighbor* and *weigh*" works well in most situations, but again the rule bends. Harry L. Arnold devised an absurd sentence containing a host of words that disobey the rule. "Neither could either weird, surfeited, counterfeit, sheik raise a stein, seize the height by stealth, or summon the leisure to make an obeisance to the seismograph on weir."

The spell-check provision on computers works well "most of the time" (a phrase well associated with spelling), but the computer cannot intuit the intention or the subtlety of a writer. It cannot make semantic judgments. Homonyms can play havoc with the usual correctness of the device.

"If I can't spell a word, how can I look it up in the dictionary?" This is a common complaint. There are two helps. It is sometimes fruitful to guess at the spelling, for the pronunciation does provide some clues. Another method is to look up a synonym; often the perplexing word will be provided. *Psychosis* will be listed as a synonym of *madness*. A thesaurus or synonym dictionaries are helpful aids for poor spellers.

Although simplified spelling plans have largely failed over the years, a major overhaul of English spelling is planned for Euro English, the accepted language of the European Union. English won over German as the common language, but not without concessions. The irregularities of English spelling were to be eliminated over a five-year period. In the first year, *c* will disappear. The *s* sound will be taken over by *s* and the *k* sound by *k*. "Sitizens kan rejois."

By the fifth year, spelling should become phonetic. This is the way one brochure put it.

> *After zis fifz yer, ve vil hav a reli sensible riten styl. Zer vil be no mor trubles or difikultis and evrivun vil find it ezi tu understand ech ozer. Ze drem vil finali kum tru.*

Will the Americans and English ever follow suit? Unlikely: We love/hate our spelling, but it's our spelling!

Enlightening postscript: by derivation, spelling is related to magic. Even today, a spell is a group of words with magical powers.

Spoonerisms

"This pie is occupewed. May I sew you to another sheet?"
—William A. Spooner

Thus did, according to legend, the Reverend Spooner show a parishioner to her seat. That transposition of initial sounds, called **spoonerism**, has, for better or worse, acquired the name of the good clergyman. He probably did say, "It is kisstiomary to cuss the bride" and "There is no peace in a home where dinner swells." He may gave told an undergraduate student, "You have tasted your worm, hissed my mystery lectures, and must catch the first town drain."

He is credited with a great variety of other delightful spoonerisms. He inquired, "Is the bean dizzy?" He liked to ride a "well-boiled icicle." At a naval review, he saw "a marvelous display of cattleships and bruisers." He told a friend, "You've quite a nosey little cook here." He scolded an undergraduate for "fighting liars in the quadrangle." Once he announced a hymn: "Kingering Congs Their Titles Take."

Spoonerisms preceded the reverend, but he made them famous and gave them a name. Perhaps most of us have created an unintentional spoonerism now and then: *cronuts and dullers, mutter and buffins, pay and spraint, mold a heeting, heed the forses, a hay of rope.*

Commentators and others have been known to create spoonerisms. A Canadian moderator said at the end of an address: "You have been listening to the Honourable Minister of Wealth and Hellfire." A weather reporter warned of "rain and slow followed by sneet." A former army major of Colorado Springs had a name famous in humor circles: Robert Spooner. True to his name, he introduced himself at a military meeting: "OK, fellows, this is Major Speaner spooking."

A spoonerism provides merriment but it somehow conveys the message.

Stereotype

*"Who's absent-minded now?" chortled the
professor to his wife as they were walking
home from church.*
*"You left your umbrella in the rack, but I
remembered both yours and mine."*
And he proudly exhibited both umbrellas.
*"But, dear," protested his wife, "Neither
of us brought an umbrella today."*
—Evan Esar-*The Comic Encyclopedia*

This is a feeble joke, but its roots go back to the ancient
Romans, Greeks, and probably beyond. The absent-minded
professor is a common **stereotype**, the butt of many jokes, which
depend on predictable characterizations. A stereotype is a plate
cast from a metal surface. The results are, of course, uniform. In
human terms, a stereotype is a mental picture held in common by
a group of people. This standardized image "represents an
oversimplified opinion, prejudiced attitude, or uncritical judgment."
"The professor may be bright, but he has this embarrassing
weakness."

A relatively good-natured side to stereotyping is found in
humor. In 206 B.C.E., the dramatist Plautus produced his play,
Miles Gloriosus, the "Braggart Soldier." The central character,
more bluster than substance, became a stereotype used by later
dramatists, even Shakespeare, who created the complex, three-
dimensional Falstaff. Falstaff is a boasting soldier, but Shakespeare
has made of him a living being, not a cardboard figure.

Other stock characters became popular: the rich old, weak-
minded man; the scolding mother-in-law; the tricky servant, brighter
than his master. Television sitcoms provide many stereotypes. The
level-headed wife and her inept husband are the parents of other
stereotypes: the lovelorn teenager, the mischievous preteen, the
wise-beyond-his-years eight-year-old. Sampling at random an

episode of any sitcom will gather up other recognizable stereotypes, provoking the expected laughs. Stereotypes abound in films as well as in television. The self-absorbed young beauty fails to recognize the sterling qualities of our hero and instead favors the reckless rogue with charm.

In life, stereotypes are not usually funny. Racial stereotypes stir up social unrest. Ethnic stereotypes, as demonstrated in Bosnia and elsewhere, have deadly results. Voters often stereotype members of the opposing party. "He/She's a Democrat/Republican and can't be trusted."

Stereotypes are insidious. The most enlightened among us may harbor a few stereotypes, even if the examples are harmless.

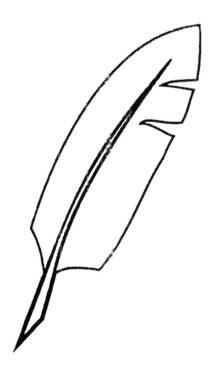

Structure Words

I'll not deny you make
A very pretty squirrel track;
Talents differ: all is well and wisely put;
If I cannot carry forests on my back,
Neither can you crack a nut.
                              —Ralph Waldo Emerson

A quarrel between the mountain and the squirrel is resolved by the squirrel when he makes the sage observation in the last two lines. The resolution of this fable depends upon two words: *if* and *neither*. Though these do not contain any messages in themselves, they glue the sentence together to make sense.

Words divide into two large groups: content words and **structure (or function) words**. Content words carry the core of meaning and structure words help content words make sense.

Content words can make sense without structure words, but not vice versa.

You easily grow beautiful roses.

The major content word groups, here illustrated, are pronoun, adverb, verb, adjective, noun. Prepositions and conjunctions have a different purpose: showing relationships. While the major job of content words is to carry the content (or meaning) of the sentence, structure words bind content words together into sentences, phrases, clauses. Content words are added easily to the language as you find new things to talk about, but new structure words are seldom introduced. They are part of the grammar of the language, the way in which words are put together to make sense. Grammar is much more stable than vocabulary. Though new structure words are introduced very rarely into the language, new vocabulary (content) words enter the language at a rapid pace as new products (like computers), experiences, and concepts are born.

Here's a simple demonstration of the importance of structure words:

After
Although
As
Because
Before
Even if
Since
Until
When
Whenever

 Essie arrived, Doug seemed happy.

We'll never know how Doug feels about Essie until we learn the structure word chosen.

Structure words are so closely integrated into English grammar that we recognize an English sentence even if we don't know all the meanings.

Two sentences demonstrate the unique strengths of structure words.

1. *Although aposiopesis has often been used for effect, excessive use of this rhetorical device cannot be countenanced.*
2. *The letter is on a corner of the table near the shelf with the dictionary.*

If we remove the nouns in the first sentence, it looks like this.

Although _____ has often been used for _____, excessive _____ of this rhetorical _____ cannot be countenanced.

A writer instantly recognizes this as an English sentence even if *aposiopesis* (break, interruption) and *countenanced* (approved) are unfamiliar. But if we remove the structure words in the second sentence, we're left with a catalogue of words rather than a recognizable English sentence.

Letter is corner table shelf dictionary.

The structure words cement the parts together.

Two types of messages cut down or omit the structure words. Telegrams are short to save money. Headlines are short to cram as much information as possible into a limited space. Sometimes the omission of structure words results in a tortured humorous headline. Misspellings, mispronunciations, and unfortunate compressions bedevil editors. Headlines are especially vulnerable to double meanings and garbled syntax. The following are some of those collected by Richard Lederer.

Motorman Well, Autopsy Reveals
Miners Refuse to Work After Death
Nonbelievers Gather to Share Their Beliefs
Million Women March Attracts Thousands
Man Struck by Lighting Faces Battery Charge
Fireproof Clothing Factory Burns to Ground
Severed Head Offers Few Answers
Plea for Cut in Prices of Free Milk
Bath Officer Shoots Man with Knife

Subjective- Objective Writing

A noiseless patient spider,
I marked where on a little promontory it stood isolated,
Marked how to explore the vacant vast surrounding,
It launched forth filament, filament, filament out of itself,
Ever unreeling them, ever tirelessly speeding them.

And you O my soul where you stand,
Surrounded, detached, in measureless oceans of space,
Ceaselessly musing, venturing, throwing, seeking the
spheres to connect them.
Till the bridge you will need be formed, ill the ductile
anchor hold,
Till the gossamer thread you fling catch somewhere,
O my soul.

—Walt Whitman

A wet spider web,
sagging from weight of raindrops
sparkles in the sun.

—Gigi Garrido

The two selections demonstrate the difference between **subjective** and **objective writing**. Walt Whitman conveys his emotions about life's meaning after observing a spider attempting to build a web. Gigi Garrido, a high school student, has created a haiku, a simple observation, without any deeper philosophizing. The first is highly subjective, especially in the second stanza. The second is simple, objective, straightforward. Similar subject matter, different approaches.

Objective writing tends to be a series of reports. It concentrates on the facts and lets the reader interpret them. Subjective writing provides the author's interpretation. There is a place for both kinds of writing.

In journalism, the news reports should be objective. Editorials and letters to the editor can be (and usually are) quite subjective. In fiction, Ernest Hemingway is noted for his spare, objective style. Poetry tends to be subjective, though the haiku is often objective, as in the haiku above.

Young writers, filled with themselves, tend to write subjectively, drawing upon their feelings, likes and dislikes. Good objective writing is sometimes more difficult. It requires a discipline that controls those excessive adjectives and adverbs.

The division between subjective and objective is not a hard-and-fast one. A writer is subjectively wrapped in his work, no matter what he is creating. Objective writing removes the *I*. Writing objectively is good training for aspiring writers.

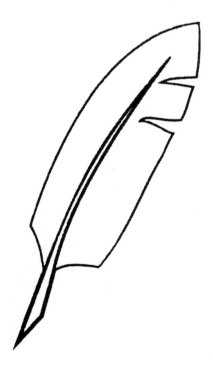

Suspense

> *There is no terror in the bang, only the anticipation of it.*
> —Alfred Hitchcock

"Make 'em laugh, Make 'em cry. Make 'em wait." This old advice to authors states the strategy of suspense as tersely as did Alfred Hitchcock. The heart of suspense is contained in its Latin roots: from *pendere*, "to hang." Suspense leaves the reader or listener "hanging." Suspense may be divided into two categories, two strategies for keeping the reader "hanging."

Detective story strategies demonstrate the differences. In the first method, the more common, a crime is committed, but the guilty person remains unknown until the end. The Hercule Poirot novels of Agatha Christie are good examples. Often, Poirot gathers all the suspects in a room and proceeds to reveal the clues that led him to the guilty person.

The second type of suspense is achieved in reverse. The story begins by showing the crime and its perpetrator. The suspense consists in the reader's or listener's attempts to guess how the detective will unravel the mystery. This is a mystery of *How?* and *Why?*, rather than a mystery of *Who?* The popular television sleuth Columbo demonstrated this strategy.

By hinting at future events, **foreshadowing** provides suspense. The opening sentence of *A Tale of Two Cities* foreshadows tragedy: It begins

> *"It was the best of times, it was the worst of times…"*

and lists the other conflicting aspects of that period. The reader knows that something bad will happen. The suspense is in not knowing who will be affected and how.

Symbols

And the rockets' red glare, the bombs
bursting in air,
Gave proof through the night that
our flag was still there.
　　　　　　　　　—Francis Scott Key

That flag, the star-spangled banner, was far more than a piece of cloth. It symbolized the hopes of the recently formed United States. **Symbols** in themselves are not "real." They stand for, represent a wide range of human activities and situations.

Symbols are powerful motivators. Religious symbols- cross, Star of David, star and crescent- have generated devotion and sometimes bloodshed. Probably the most hated symbol ever is the Nazi swastika, associated with the horrendous crimes of Adolf Hitler and the Third Reich.

Symbols are especially prominent at holiday times. A baby clad only in a cloth is a symbol of the New Year. A poinsettia, holly wreath, and a balsam tree represent Christmas. A skeleton, witch's hat, and a ghostly figure are symbols of Halloween. The candles of the Menorah symbolize Hanukkah.

Companies seek to provide recognizable logos as symbols, thus providing a subtle nonverbal message to potential customers; for example, that uniquely designed swirl, called the *swoosh*, is identified with Nike. Recognizable visual symbols are taken in at a glance and are not dependent upon language.

Misunderstanding of the part played by symbols results in comments like these.

I am not amazed at the ability of science
to measure size, distance, and brightness of
the stars. What puzzles me is how scientists
found out the names of the stars.

Pigs are properly named. They are such dirty animals.

The name Ruth doesn't suit my sister. She's more of a Tiffany.

Ice is appropriately named. It's such a cold word.

Finally, this old joke that contains a bit of insight about symbols:

"Your house is not legally in Minnesota. This survey puts it twenty yards over the Iowa line."
"Really? That's wonderful. Now I won't have any more of those cold Minnesota winters."

Words themselves are symbols.

Synecdoche

*Then shall ye bring down my gray hairs
with sorrow to the grave.*

—Genesis

Here the gray hairs refer to the patriarch Jacob. **Synecdoche** substitutes a part for the whole or the whole for the part: the *hairs* for *Jacob*. Despite its forbidding name, synecdoche is a fairly common language practice. When Einstein is called a *brain*, the entire Albert is intended, not just the physical organ. Examples of body synecdoches include the *Nose* (Jimmy Durante), the *Toe* (a successful place kicker in football), the *Arm* (a baseball pitcher) hired *hands* (employees), *Muscles* (an athlete), and a *private eye*. "You're all *heart*" is another example.

Apart from the body, synecdoche appears in forty *head* of cattle, twenty *sail*, and the *army* (a soldier). When restaurants advertise for smiling *faces*, they want cheerful employees, intact.

Synonyms

How weary, stale, flat, and unprofitable
Seem to me all the uses of this world.
—William Shakespeare

When Hamlet in this soliloquy expresses his dissatisfaction with this world, he uses four synonyms to express his despair. Though they are indeed synonyms, they display a truth about synonyms: they differ slightly from each other. *Stale* and *flat* are closest, but even these can be discriminated.

The columnist James J. Kilpatrick devoted a fascinating column to the difference between *wiggle* and *wriggle*. Do you wiggle (wriggle) your toes? Kilpatrick consulted many dictionaries, including the eleven volume *Oxford English Dictionary*, and finally decided that though the words are close in meaning, there are differences. He suggests that *wriggle* connotes a circular motion while *wiggle* suggests a motion side to side or up and down! Close, but different. The surefire test is using each in the same context. The winner in a philosophical argument might obnoxiously say, "You can't wriggle out of that one." *Wiggle* just doesn't fit here.

Sidebar: the *wr* in wriggle is a clue. It suggests *twisted*, *turning*; *convulsive*. Other *wr* words with the same flavor are *writhe*, *wry*, *wrest*, and *wrong*.

Synonyms are words that "have the same or nearly the same meaning." This is the dictionary definition accepted by all users of language, but it is suspect. Finding a pair of words that may be used interchangeably in all situations is probably impossible. Words have connotations and denotations. Pairs of synonyms may have practically the same denotations, but connotations are a different matter. *Imitate* is a synonym of *copy*. Both *imitate* and *copy* mean "to reproduce the style or characteristic of something." As actually used, however, the words go off in different directions. We can *imitate* or *copy* a person's mannerisms, but we *copy*, not *imitate*, a document to be duplicated. Even the closest synonyms have unique connotation unavailable to the other word in the pair. *Family* and *kin* have the same denotations but vary in use. *Famous* and *renowned* are synonyms, but *renowned* is a more positive word. *Pick* and *choose* are synonyms, but *choose* is the broader term.

The narrower the word meanings, the closer the synonyms. The broader meanings allow for diversity. *Cold* and *frigid* are synonyms, but the numerous associated meanings of *cold* make it much more general and inclusive than *frigid*. On the other hand, *inexorable* and *remorseless* have narrower meanings, but even they are distinguishable, not interchangeable. Both suggest *relentlessness*, but *remorseless* adds the suggestion of cruelty.

Even very close synonyms are not interchangeable. Someone once suggested *raveled* and *unraveled* as perfect interchangeable synonyms, yet Shakespeare's line would lose its effect if *unraveled* were substituted in *Macbeth* for *raveled*: "Sleep that knits up the unraveled sleeve of care." Nor would Sherlock Holmes *ravel* a mystery in the last page. *Backward* and *backwards* seem just about identical. William Safire pointed out that you can move backward or backwards, but you can only bend over *backward*. You can't sneak a *backwards* glance.

Syntax

I met a traveler from an antique land
Who said: "Two vast and trunkless legs of stone
Stand in the desert...Near them, on the sand,
Half sunk, a shattered visage lies, whose frown,
And wrinkled lip, and sneer of cold command
Tell that its sculptor well those passions read
Which yet survive, stamped on these lifeless things,
The hand that mocked them, and the heart that fed;
And on the pedestal these words appear;
'My name is Ozymandias, king of kings;
Look on my works, ye Mighty and despair!'
Nothing beside remains. Round the decay
Of that colossal wreck, boundless and bare
The lone and level sands stretch far away."
—Percy Bysshe Shelley

In his poem "Ozymandias," Shelley expressed the vanity of human wishes in a tight 14-line stanza. The first eight lines, here quoted, tell an ironic story of a cruel and powerful king and an unimportant artist he scorned. It is the unimportant artist, however, who has the last word. The story is all there, but it must be derived from the structure of the sentence beginning with line 3. Only when we realize that the direct objects of *survive* are *hand* and *heart*, do we begin to understand what the poet is implying. When we realize that *them* refers to *passions*, then we fully understand what the poet is suggesting.

In this scenario, the king's miserable qualities have been captured in stone by the lowly artist. It is the artist's *hand* and the king's *heart* that have survived down the ages. The *frown*, *wrinkled lip*, and *sneer* have all been captured in stone.

What makes "Ozymandias" a candidate for misinterpretation is the sentence structure. The poet has changed the normal word order: "well those passions read" instead of "read those passions well." He has separated *survive* from its objects, leaving the word *survive* apparently dangling. He has separated a pronoun and its antecedents: *them...passions*. The result is challenging compression and a satisfying leap of understanding when the structure is understood.

The previous paragraph has explored the syntax of the sentence. **Syntax** is a forbidding term for a simple concept: the structure of a sentence, how a sentence is put together to communicate.

Syntax consists of two elements: word order and morphology. Word order presents few problems. Even when the order is changed somewhat, as for emphasis— "Mexican food I really enjoy"— the meaning is clear and usage acceptable. Yet word order easily allows subtle distinctions difficult to manage through morphological changes. In the sentence "Elaine loves Jerry," insertion of only at various spots in the sentence affects the meaning critically.

The other syntactical element, morphology, deals with word formation, inflections that signal meaning while changing spelling, word endings, or changes within the word itself. *Rang* is an inflectional change of *ring*; *diamonds*, of *diamond*; and *theirs*, of *their*.

Though English has lost many inflections, some still remain...to bedevil students, who must learn that *between you and I* is incorrect. The object form *me* is needed after *between*. Pronouns especially have retained inflections: for example, *I- me*; *she- her*; *he- him*; *they- them*. An exception: the second-person pronoun has lost the singular form in everyday secular speech: thou. *You* now is used for singular and plural.

Nouns avoid some of the complications. *Between you and John* avoids the perilous *I- me*.

English verb inflections still signal tense. Note how Chinese, an uninflected language, suggests changes in tense without changing the form of the verb:

English	Chinese
They write	*they this day write*
They wrote	*they past day write*
They will write	*they next day write*
They have written	*they write finish*

English sometimes requires clarifiers:

> *"I put my faith in Fred."*

Since *put* is a verb that doesn't change form in denoting tenses, the preceding example is ambiguous. We need a qualifier to tell whether *put* is in the present or the past tense.

"I now put my faith in Fred." (present)
"I then put my faith in Fred." (past)

Though English relies principally upon word order and qualifiers to communicate, it still has remnants of an earlier, highly inflected day, a heritage from its Germanic origins. Mario Pei has said, "Learning to speak English is generally easier for a Norwegian than for a Pole or Spaniard." Like English, Norwegian is a Germanic language. Polish is Slavic and Spanish, Romance.

English has come a long way. It is the only Germanic language that doesn't inflect adjectives. In English, adjectives are invariable, no matter where in the sentence they occur.

Some linguistics theorize that English might have lost most or all inflections in time. A comparison of modern English with Chaucer reveals many now-discarded inflections. Perhaps the invention of printing from movable type froze the pesky *I- me* in its present form, even as a word like *thou* was disappearing.

English-speaking students have little trouble with word order, but those inflectional errors like *have sang, we seen, I done* are still around to plague us!

Topsy-Turvy

There are two tragedies in life. One is to
lose your heart's desire. The other is to gain it.
—George Bernard Shaw

Some writers have the ability to turn things upside down, **topsy-turvy**, to give a better perspective on some aspect of living. In the preceding quotation, Shaw turns upside down the usual cliché, the second sentence in the quotation. The third sentence catches the reader unaware and pleases by its unexpected insight. Shaw delighted in topsy-turvy, as in these quotations.

A lifetime of happiness: No man alive could
bear it. It would be hell on earth.

The worst sin towards our fellow creatures is
not to hate them, but to be indifferent to them:
that's the essence of inhumanity.

The more things a man is ashamed of, the more
respectable he is.

A film depicting a period in the life of Gilbert and Sullivan was called *Topsy-Turvy*, because that is the distinguishing feature of W.S. Gilbert's prose. In the Lord Admiral's song in *H.M.S. Pinafore*, he captures this quality perfectly.

Stick close to your desks and never go to sea
and you all may be Rulers of the Queen's
Navee.

Or as the Grand Inquisitor says in *The Gondoliers*,

When everyone is somebody, then no one's
anybody!

No writer ever understood topsy-turvy better than Oscar Wilde. Lady Bracknell, in *The Importance of Being Earnest*, is a treasure house of upside-down logic. When she questions Jack, her prospective son-in-law, she asks if he knows everything or nothing. When he replies, "I know nothing," she is delighted.

> *I do not approve of anything that tampers with natural ignorance. Ignorance is like a delicate exotic fruit; touch it and the bloom is gone. The whole theory of modern education is radically unsound. Fortunately, in England, at any rate, education produces no effect whatsoever. If it did, it would prove a serious danger to the upper classes and probably lead to acts of violence in Grosvenor Square.*

The great satirists have always used topsy-turvy to shock and stimulate. Jonathan Swift's "Modest Proposal," discussed in the entry on "Satire," is one of the strongest and most successful uses of topsy-turvy to shock.

Translation

Poesy is of so subtle a spirit, that in pouring out of one Language into another, it will all evaporate.

—Sir John Denham

More than 300 years ago, in translating the *Aeneid*, Denham realized how deceptively difficult translation can be. A French-English dictionary, for example apparently provides a French word for each English word and an English word for each French word. But the neat columns of definitions are deceptive. Words from different languages do not match perfectly in connotation and denotation. Even English synonyms are not interchangeable.

Corresponding words in two languages are separated culturally and historically from becoming perfect matches. Richard Howard, famous translator of the French novelist Marcel Proust, once confessed, "There are days when translation does seem impossible, when the English word *bread* and the French word *pain* seem to be only absurd equivalents." The Greek word *tyrannos* has no exact English equivalent. The Greek play *Oedipus Tyrannos* has been translated *Oedipus the King*, but *king* is inadequate.

Strangely enough, a strictly literal translation, which painstakingly tries to represent each word accurately, may be less true to the original than a looser translation more in keeping with the spirit of the original. No translation can be 100% faithful to the original text.

Idioms are especially troublesome in translation. In the movie *Casablanca*, Humphrey Bogart says to Ingrid Bergman, "Here's looking at you, kid." When the translator for French audiences tried to provide French captions, he often found it impossible to catch the nuances of the American idioms. Bogart's toast was especially troublesome. The caption writer decided to provide a simple expression that caught something of the idiom's flavor: *Bonne chance*! Good luck! A literal translation of the toast would have been ludicrous. Not a single word in the toast can be literally translated. At least *bonne chance* captured some of its spirit.

Humor can often be found in "English" notices in foreign countries.

A Czech tourist brochure advised. "Take one of your horse-driven city tours—we guarantee no miscarriages."

A Polish traffic sign directed, "Right turn toward immediate outside."

An elevator sign in a Romanian hotel read, "This lift is being fixed for the next days. During that time we regret that you will be unbearable."

A sign in an Italian doctors office announced, "Specialist in Women's and Other Diseases."

Before we commend ourselves on our greater sophistication, consider how we might mangle a sign in Swedish for Scandinavian visitors.

Mark Twain was aware of the difficulties of translation and had fun with the process. His sketch "The Jumping Frog" was translated into French. Then Twain took the French translation and translated it back to English, quite literally as you'll see.

Original Version- *Well, there was a feller here once by the name of Jim Smiley, in the winter of '49- or maybe it was the spring of '50- I don't recollect exactly.*

Retranslated from the French- *It there was one time here an individual known under the name of Jim Smiley; it was in the winter of '49, possibly well at the spring of '50, I no me recollect exactly.*

And this is uncomplicated prose!

240

Usage

The grammar has a rule absurd
Which I could call an outworn myth:
A preposition is a word
You mustn't end a sentence with!
—Berton Braley

Grammar is the underlying structure of a language. **Usage** is what people say it is. Grammar alters very slowly, usage, more rapidly. Usage concerns itself with language etiquette. It changes. An acceptable language convention of the past may be unacceptable today. Shakespeare uses the double superlative, "the most unkindest cut of all." Modern usage frowns upon it.

An interesting story involves the avoidance of ending a sentence with a preposition. Long believed to be a "rule," the practice has been happily overlooked by major writers for centuries. Winston Churchill derided the unnatural results with this comment: "This is the sort of English up with which I will not put."

In the following pairings, the supposedly "correct" sentence seems unnatural.

"Who's the girl with whom you went?"
"Who's the girl you went with?"

Sally is the one to whom I went to give this book.
Sally is the girl I want to give this book to.

Usage is sometimes divided into various levels, each level associated with a particular group or occasion. In the preceding paired sentences, the relaxed sentence is more colloquial.

Formal, or literary, English uses words and expressions seldom found in ordinary conversation. Serious articles, formal presentations, sermons—all use formal English. Here's a sample of words used in formal English but rarely in conversation:

autonomy, duplicity, allegation, environs, gratuity.

Informal English has several labels. **Colloquial English** is essentially the language of conversation. It is more relaxed, spontaneous, more prone to contractions like *I'll, you're,* and *they've.* It tends to the use of simpler words than those used in formal English: *trickery* for *charlatanism, heavy* for *ponderous, sky* for *firmament, try* for *endeavor.* Colloquial English concentrates on words of Anglo-Saxon origin. A word count of formal English would show more words of Latin and Greek origin than those used in average conversations.

Colloquial English is not limited to conversation. It is often used in books and popular magazines. The style of this book is a blend of formal and informal English, an indication that the divisions are not hard and fast.

Slang has been called "the poetry of the streets," language at its most exuberant. Many of our colorful words originated as slang and gradually worked their way into the dictionaries and standard vocabulary. *Fun, stingy,* and *clever* started life as slang and soon filled a need. Many words of slang origin are colorful, adding zest to language. Is there a colorful synonym to match *skinflint*? The more recent *skinhead* entered the language in 1953 and stayed there. *Highfalutin* became respectable even earlier, in 1839. Does *pompous* as effectively capture that irritating quality?

Slang's strength contains the seeds of its weakness. Its very flair and color soon weary its users. As a result, much slang is short-lived, incomprehensible to a later generation. One of the most widespread of all slang words was *twenty-three,* a strange word giving a general meaning of approval. It has long since disappeared. Ponderous dictionaries list thousands of slang words that had their fifteen minutes of fame and then faded, words like *hunky-dory.*

Music and other forms of pop culture generate many new slang words, but like a fashion wardrobe, slang vocabulary has to be refurbished every season. It's a fascinating challenge to guess which slang words will persevere.

Word Magic

Double, double toil and trouble;
Fire burn and cauldron bubble.
                                    —William Shakespeare

The witches in *Macbeth* have stirred up an appetizing brew of snake, newt, toe of frog, tongue of dog, and other unspeakable ingredients. Their incantation returns to the refrain quoted above. There is magic in the potpourri; all is accompanied by the chant.

Words have been accorded magical qualities since ancient times. The importance of names is treated elsewhere in this book, but the fascination with language magic extends to all words. Charms, magical spells, incantations have misled the hopeful since the first "wizard" appeared to heal the sick, encourage the hopeless, and confound the enemy.

An interesting word, *abracadabra*, goes back to Gnostics, a 2nd century C.E. religious sect, who believed that the word calls upon benevolent spirits and wards off disease. The word was arranged like this and carried in an amulet:

ABRACADABRA
ABRACADABR
ABRACADAB
ABRACADA
ABRACAD
ABRACA
ABRAC
ABRA
ABR
AB
A

Abracadabra eventually lost its religious significance and became a general word for charm.

Magic appears in literature. A charming (ah, that word!) example is John Wellington Wells, the central character of Gilbert and Sullivan's operetta *The Sorcerer*. In his opening song, Wells sums up his bag of tricks and in so doing describes the stock-in-trade of modern dealers in word magic.

> *Oh! My name is John Wellington Wells,*
> *I'm a dealer in magic and spells,*
> *In blessings and curses*
> *And ever-filled purses*
> *In prophecies, witches, and knells.*

W.S. Gilbert provides the usual confusions. Wells produces a love philtre that reaches the wrong partners. To right the ensuing wrongs, Wells himself must pay the penalty.

Of course, word magic is especially prominent in advertising. Certain magic words appear over and over: *free, genuine, original, rewards, home-grown, garden-fresh, eye-catching*. Does *émincé de poulet* taste better than *chicken hash*? Does *Wildwood Heights* sound like a more inviting home investment than *Burton Acres*?